breathe
yoga for teens

breathe
yoga for teens

written by
mary kaye chryssicas

photography by
angela coppola

DK Publishing

LONDON, NEW YORK, MUNICH,
MELBOURNE, AND DELHI

editor elizabeth hester
managing art director michelle baxter
designer jessica park
publishing director beth sutinis
art director dirk kaufman
production ivor parker
dtp kathy farias
photographer angela coppola

First American Edition, 2007
Published in the United States by DK Publishing
375 Hudson Street, New York, New York 10014

07 08 09 10 11 10 9 8 7 6 5 4 3 2 1

DK books are available at special discounts when
purchased in bulk for sales promotions, premiums,
fund-raising, or educational use. For details, contact:
DK Publishing Special Markets
375 Hudson Street, New York, New York 10014
SpecialSales@dk.com

A catalog record for this book is available
from the Library of Congress.

ISBN-13 978-0-7566-2661-7

Reproduced by Colourscan,
Singapore
Printed and bound in China
by Leo Paper Products Ltd.

Discover more at
www.dk.com

contents

Publisher's note

Safety First: Not all exercises are suitable for everyone, and some may result in injury if not properly performed. Any user of this book assumes the risks of injury which may arise in connection with the exercises or advice in this book. Consult with your doctor before beginning a new exercise program or if you have any questions about the suitability of these exercises for your particular needs or medical condition.

All that we are is the result of

what we have thought.

The mind is everything.

What we think we become.

Buddha, founder of Buddhism
c. 563 BCE – c. 483 BCE

why yoga?

In high school, I was your typical teen: energetic, overbooked, boy crazy, and anxious. On top of that, I was self conscious about my weight, preoccupied with friendships, worried about grades, and embarrassed by my parents (who thought nothing of fitting my chipped front tooth with a silver cap—thanks for the memories!). In short, I was a perfect candidate for yoga. It wasn't until years later that I finally gave yoga a try. I was hooked. I could feel the way yoga helped my body and mind become stronger than they ever were. I loved that I wasn't expected to compete. I could do yoga and feel confident and calm.

Now that I teach yoga, my teen classes are my favorites. I remember my teen years so vividly, and I love to see what a difference yoga can make. Teens today have even more on their plates, with super-competitive academics and sports, packed schedules, and parental pressure. The kids in my classes use their yoga practice to chill out and get in tune with their bodies. Their patience grows, their posture improves, their confidence shines, their energy increases, their minds become peaceful, and their stress levels decrease. One of the greatest signs that yoga is working is simply laughter—when yogis are free from worry, they freely smile, laugh, and enjoy life. Isn't that what it's all about?

history of yoga

Yoga means union. The word "yoga" comes from the Sanskrit word yuj, meaning to yoke or bind together. In this togetherness, the mind, body, and breath are one, working together to give you peace of mind and strength in body and joyful spirit.

The exact story behind the birth of yoga is a real mystery, but that's part of why people are drawn to this practice. What we do know is that clay figures and cave drawings depict humans in yoga poses thousands of years ago; yoga stands the test of time.

Early yoga focused mainly on seated poses for meditation. Then people who practiced yoga, called yogis, added more active poses. Poses were based on the movements and postures of animals and objects in nature. Yogis thought that by

imitating these animals, they might take on the strength of a lion, the stamina of a camel, or the steadiness of a still tree in a storm. They knew for sure that when they tried poses like Tree or Downward Dog, they felt great afterward.

In modern yoga studios, you'll find several different forms of yoga practiced. I usually follow the Ashtanga tradition, but I also borrow from Iyengar and Kundalini in my classes. There's really no right or wrong style of yoga since most of the poses are the same, and all yoga practices have the same purpose: to join body, mind, and spirit while opening the heart.

Let it be

There's a long history to yoga— and there's also a long history of teens magnifying their problems. Girls are always testing friendships, and not always in the kindest ways. As long as you treat others as you wish to be treated, you are doing your part. Try not to be bothered when you don't get invited to the party or someone is unkind to you. Think of it as the other person's problem; don't ask why or pretend to care. It's their loss. Let it be...

who does yoga?

Someone who practices yoga is called a yogi. You can be a yogi no matter who you are. It's not exclusive. It's not a club. There's no "good" at yoga. Some people are stronger than they are flexible, and for others it's the reverse. But none of that ever matters because you have to start somewhere! All yogis have to practice, but anyone can benefit from yoga.

athletes: Think yoga is only for hippies? Think again. Extraordinary athletes like Kareem Abdul-Jabbar relied on yoga for training—once he started practicing yoga, he had no muscle injuries during his basketball career. Maria Sharapova does yoga to maximize her performance on the tennis court and protect her hips from injury.

people who need healing: People who suffer from scoliosis, cancer, depression, carpal tunnel syndrome, arthritis, cerebral palsy, ADD, ADHD, and other ailments benefit from yoga. In fact, many cancer doctors recommend yoga now as preventative medicine.

bendy people: Flexible people like dancers and gymnasts already have a wide range of motion and can access energy and calm by what's called a "moving meditation." Yoga helps add strength to the mix, balancing flexibility and power.

yoga and sports

When I taught the Harvard Rugby team, they turned into yogis after the first tree pose. They all tried so hard, grunting, puffing, and falling. Not surprisingly, power poses such as Crow come easily to them. But balance poses like Eagle and Dancer's Pose are more challenging. Yoga offers athletes something that no sport can give them. Not only does it help prevent injuries (as pro football teams with yoga programs are proving), it also has a unique spiritual and mental connection that can improve your game and your life.

stiff people: I often hear, "I can't do yoga! I can't even bend over." You are my dream student! People with limited flexibility can change a stiff stagger to a graceful stride with the supple spine and open hips that yoga can create. Yoga can ease your aches and pains and give you tremendous confidence in your body's abilities, to boot.

young people: Babies love yoga! I use to lay my babies on their changing table and bicycle their little legs to release gas. It wasn't a pleasant process, but it sure did relieve the pressure. Lots of yoga poses—like happy baby and child's pose—are modeled after the way young children move their bodies, so kids are natural yogis.

old people: Nursing homes are starting to employ yoga teachers. Even people in a wheel chair can reach to the sky in Lightning Bolt. Older yogis love how it activates tired muscles and sends energy soaring through the fingertips. It takes more effort, but they can all benefit from gentle yoga stretches. Don't let granny give up! Teach her a pose or two.

teens: I wish I had discovered yoga as a teen! Boy, are you lucky. Yoga has the power to help you get past all the stress, anxiety, girlfriend and boyfriend troubles, divorce, homework disasters, or the death of a close friend or relative. Because the hormones are raging inside you, your reactions may sometimes be extreme or inconsistent. Yoga teaches you how to respond to situations with a calm coolness and helps you love being you. You might connect with the spirit inside you and be smarter about the choices you make.

yoga as a way of life

The mental and spiritual sides of yoga go beyond the studio.

I have met shy teens that had trouble looking me in the eye or speaking directly to me during their first class. There is no greater reward than seeing that same teen come out of her shell and begin to laugh and talk with other kids in class. I see tall girls hunch over and hide in those first few weeks. Slowly, they see the benefits of sitting and standing tall, and their personality begins to shine through.

Yoga can be a very personal practice, but it's also about being a positive force in the universe. By taking care of each other, we make others feel good about themselves, which in turn makes you feel good. Yoga encourages you to spread kindness and positive thoughts in all you do.

Yoga helps you channel emotions so that you can be fully present. It's natural for your mind to wander with all sorts of judgments and thought patterns. But when you can focus on the breath and eliminate the chatter in your mind, you can start to become fully present, living in the moment. It's not as easy as it sounds, but like a lot of yoga's lessons, it's an important skill for getting the most out of your yoga workout as well as your life.

from Mary Kaye's diary

One day at Virginia Beach, my friend and I struck up a conversation with a kind, muscular guy sitting near us. We hung out most of the day, exchanging stories, writing poetry, and eating blueberry pie. Eventually, we learned that he was Muhammad Ali, the famous boxer. Despite his high profile, he had spent a whole day with some kids who had no idea who he was. He was just a relaxed, ordinary, modest person. Today's athletes and celebrities seem to live in a different world from their fans, when really they are much like everyone else. Celebrity star gazing has reached obsessive proportions. Find a way of life that makes you the star of your dreams.

namaste

Anjali Mudra is a sacred hand position where the palms draw together at the center line of your body. This simple yet powerful gesture is often done while saying "Namaste" but is also used in yoga poses such as Mountain, Tree, and Lotus. Anjali Mudra helps you feel centered.

mountain pose

yoga tenets

ahimsa (nonharming): treating others with compassion and helping those in need. It's also about not harming yourself.

satya (truth): carefully choosing words that do good and no harm. Be honest in all that you do. You will gain tremendous respect.

asteya (no cheating or stealing): honoring the rights of others. If you like what someone has done, credit them. People are happy to share ideas if you give them credit.

brahmacharya (self restraint): practicing self-control and being respectful of others and your body. Do not let anyone use you for your body.

aparigraha (non-attachment): avoiding materialism. Be open to change and adaptable to new situations.

santosha (acceptance): accepting who you are and those around you. Try not to judge others by the way they talk, what they wear, or who they spend time with. Everyone deserves a chance.

saucha (purity): keeping your body clean and free of toxins like smoking and drinking. Why not stay alive?

svadhyaya (clarity): being self aware and reflective of mistakes. Accept that we all make mistakes and resolve to learn from them.

tapas (ambition): doing your best with positive energy. Always try your best, but not if it means taking people down to achieve your goals. Support your friends.

ishvara pranidhana (devotion to a greater source): believing that there is meaning to the world due to a greater power.

"If you are not getting as much from life as you want to, then examine the state of your enthusiasm."

—Norman Vincent Peale, preacher and writer (1898–1993)

creating energy

Energy can send you soaring! Energy creates enthusiasm, and helps wake up your body and mind in the morning. We all know how hard it is to wake up for school and try to eat breakfast and catch a bus. Getting your body moving is a must if you want to get anything done. But it's also important to wake up your brain so you are ready to face whatever surprises come your way. And there will be surprises!

Most yoga poses are energetic poses—they require energy to master, but they give energy back, too. Your hands are reaching and sending energy up through the spine just as your feet, pressing into the mat, send energy up through your legs. Energy helps you feel present and alive and prepares you to accomplish any project or goal. It helps you feel rested so you can take on new challenges. Meet your life with enthusiasm. Your energy comes from within.

finding the breath

Although your body will accomplish all kinds of crazy things in your yoga practice, the breath is actually the most important tool you'll have. People who don't know yoga think this is bizarre. Sports like swimming and sprinting have special techniques to help you breathe, but breathing is just a means to the end of the race. Yoga begins and ends with the breath. The breath is the engine that powers it all, so we usually focus off and on throughout class with reminders on breathing techniques. When you first begin a yoga practice, you rely on helpful reminders to breathe until it becomes habit.

Everyone assumes breathing is simple since, after all, we were born breathing. However, most people don't realize that they breathe too quickly or hold their breath when faced with difficult tasks. Many of us have shallow breathing patterns, especially when stressed. Yoga teaches you how to breathe fully through tough situations, which helps you stay focused and in control, and makes problems easier to handle.

child's pose

With the body at rest, Child's Pose is the perfect place to focus on your breath. Gently sit back on your heels and fold forward. Reach your arms out forward or rest them behind you. Your forehead rests on the mat. You can actually feel the spine lengthen. Child's Pose calms the mind—try it any time you need a break.

child's pose

Let your bottom rest on the heels ----▷

"The breath is the intelligence of the body."

–T.K.V. Desikachar, yogi (1938-)

fuel the body

Yoga is never about holding the breath. Breathing fuels the body to hold poses longer and has the power to inhale goodness and exhale toxins. If breathing is difficult in a certain yoga pose, modify the pose until it feels more manageable. You should be able to breathe freely and even laugh. There is always another version of a yoga pose— let your breath help you find the one that's right for your body and flexibility level.

Can you feel your heart beat?

Relax the neck

The hands are relaxed, palms down

Rest your forehead on the floor or a block

breathing techniques

Once you've gotten used to the feel of breathing deeply, you can try some specialized breathing techniques to develop your awareness of the breath even further. Your mind is in charge of directing the breath—but that doesn't mean the rest of you can't pitch in, too. Your hands can help direct the breath one nostril at a time. You can experiment with breathing through your nose and mouth at different rates. Contract your stomach muscles to push the breath out with more control. What feels best to you? See if you can mellow out just by focusing on the breath for a while. Take your time—this relaxing exercise can be just as beneficial as the trickiest twists. It's one of the best parts about yoga: the breath naturally calms the mind. You don't need a pill.

Press the right thumb to the right nostril and inhale eight counts

Feel the belly expand and contract to drive the breath

alternate nostril breathing

Mouth closed

Hand is in mudra
position, with
the first two
fingers bent

The legs are
in Easy Pose

breathing techniques

alternate nostril breathing

Settle into a seated position. Press your right middle and pointer fingers against the palm of your right hand. Now press your right thumb to the side of your right nostril as you inhale through your left nostril for eight counts. Clamp both nostrils shut (using the thumb and ring finger) and retain the breath. Release the thumb and count to eight as you exhale through your right nostril. Repeat on the other side, using the ring finger to close off the left nostril.

ujjayi breathing

Sit comfortably in easy pose. Inhale deeply and then exhale with your mouth open as if you are fogging up a mirror. Now try to exhale with the mouth closed. Your breath should sound like the waves of the ocean. In correct ujjayi breathing, air is drawn in and out from the back of the throat and out through the nostrils. Avoid sniffing; breathe deeply.

breath of fire

Place a block or two under your bottom and straighten your back in a comfortable but active seated pose. Place your hands on your hips as you slowly inhale as much breath as possible. Then release the breath in 20 short puffs. Contract the belly to help expel the breath.

humming-bee breath

Choose any seated position to try this comforting technique. Bring your attention inward as you inhale through your nose. Make sure the inhalation is slow and long. As you exhale through your nose, make a soft humming sound in the mouth. Then just sit quietly and enjoy a peaceful moment.

chakras

Ever have writer's block? Can't stop eating cookie dough? Heartbroken over a relationship? If you went through a break up, your Anahata chakra may need some healing. (Backbends can help.) If someone close to you dies and you start to doubt your faith, your Sahasrara chakra is probably empty. (Try Savasana.)

The seven chakras are your hidden spiritual energy centers. Though they are located in the "aura," or your spiritual being, there is a physical connection between the chakras and the endocrine gland system, which runs from the base of the spine to the crown of the head. The chakras can become unbalanced and shift depending on how you feel both physically and emotionally. Sometimes events in your life will knock your chakras out of whack. Just remember that it happens to the best of us. That off-balance, slightly crazy feeling is perfectly natural—and it's something that you can improve, without the aid of a single cookie.

In yoga, the chakras have meaning for your emotional, psychological, and spiritual health. Practicing yoga can help shift imbalances and clear the energy in chakras that are blocked or out of balance. The more balanced your body and mind, the sooner you'll be able to bounce back up when life knocks you down.

intuition

Learn to trust your intuition and value that internal voice. Ever think of a particular friend just as the phone rings—then you answer the phone, and it's her? That's your intuition, or sixth sense. It can help you steer clear of danger or decide to take a chance. Some people have a hard time trusting their intuition, but it gets easier if you pay attention and start to notice patterns. Diagnosing out-of-whack chakras is intuitive—you have to listen to your own body and mind.

Legs are in Lotus Pose ----▷

Sahasrara (crown): universal spirit

Ajna (brow): intuition, understanding of self

lotus pose

Vishuddhi (throat): inner truth, your message

Anahata (heart): love, compassion

Manipura (solar plexus): stamina, willpower, well-being

Hyana mudra
(meditative
hand
gesture)

Svadhisthana (sacral): sexuality, creativity

Muladhara (root): independence, integrity, human interaction, connection to the earth

"It's not what happens to you,
but how you react to it
that matters."

–Epictetus, Phrygian philosopher (c. 55–135 CE)

warm up

Is it the way you look...or the way you look at the world? It's all in your attitude. Go into a new adventure knowing that it will be a positive experience, and the hour you spend in class or the day you spend with a new friend will be much more rewarding. Think of your life and yoga as a journey, not something you must get done because it's a race.

Warming up at the beginning of class gets your body and mind in the mood for one part of that journey. The mood is peaceful and slow while the body starts to release the stress of the day and get ready for yoga. Become aware of your breath and feel your muscles relax and prepare. Most importantly, open your mind and get ready to act with positive energy.

om: focus the mind

The sound of Om is the sound of the universe at peace. It is the feeling of euphoria, joy, peace, and stillness. It celebrates life and the world of nature and people. It brings you into the present. It's also soothing for the senses. Yogis use the sound Om to get into a frame of mind to focus in their practice. It can be used at any time—the beginning of practice, at the end, or smack dab in the middle. Whenever your class does a chant, give it a try. It might seem a little weird at first, but it's a really cool part of the yoga experience.

Chanting Om several times at the beginning or end of your practice should be calming; it sets the tone for class. You'll begin by taking a big inhale and chanting the sound of Om, which actually breaks down into three sounds: A-O-M. As you start to exhale, make the ah sound followed by the oh sound and ending with mmmm.

seated prayer pose

Feet are planted firmly on the floor

Take a short break before inhaling again and repeating the same pattern three times: ah, oh, mmmm. Try it softly if chanting feels awkward at first. As you become more comfortable in class, it will get easier and become effortless.

Remember that Om is considered a sacred sound, so try not to laugh. It's also a chance for you to feel connected with other yogis in the group. So open up and let your practice begin!

be present

At the beginning of class, I ask everyone to send out kind thoughts to the people on the mats around them. When you're sending out positive energy, it truly creates a happy environment in which to practice. Nothing is worse than a yoga class with competitiveness and tension. If you feel that tension in class, try to forgive everyone around you and reset your mind in a positive way. Let go of that comment or action that made you doubt your friend or stung your pride. Anyone can hold a grudge, but it takes someone special to forgive.

— Press your knees open with your elbows

seated prayer pose

Take your feet wider than shoulder-width apart and squat down. Sink into your hips, feet flat on the mat. (If your heels do not touch the mat, try sitting on a block.) Take your hands to prayer position at your heart and press your elbows against the inner points of your knees.

"Om! This syllable is the whole world. The past, the present, the future—everything is just the word Om."

— *Swami Krishnananda, from* Mandukya Upanishad

easy does it

Ease into your yoga practice, jump into life. It's OK to take your time to assess new opportunities and feel your way into new experiences. Just don't get caught up in analyzing every detail, or wait until you can do something to perfection before giving it a try. You can't learn without making mistakes. Some people need to make more mistakes than others—but don't be too hard on yourself when you do something that doesn't live up to your standards. Just try to find the humor in it and jump back up and try again. If your pose looks weird, try again. It will get easier. Everything does with practice. There's something about Butterfly Pose that always has me imagining where I would fly if I could go

Drop the shoulders as the spine reaches straight up

This feels great in the hips!

butterfly pose

Let the knees flop open

anywhere. Let your warm-up poses open up your mind as you sink into your breath. We jump into a lot of activities without thoughtfully preparing our mind. It's OK to slow down, regroup, and find focus.

There are lots of great ways to ease into your yoga practice. Find the poses you like best to ease those hips open, loosen the hamstrings, and create stillness in your mind to prepare you physically and mentally for your yoga practice.

from Mary Kaye's diary

When I was young, I was painfully shy (which everyone reminds me is soooo hard to believe). I was so shy that my parents sent me to meet with my teachers and a school psychologist to help me come out of my shell. They were concerned that I was too quiet and afraid to participate. And I was. I was afraid of rejection, not having the perfect response, doing something wrong. But I also just wanted to watch and ease into my life. I would jump in when I was ready…and boy did I ever!

forward bend

Bring your navel toward ----▷ your thighs

Legs are flat on the floor and straight ahead

persevere

Downward Dog is a great beginning and transitional pose that you will come back to again and again. It's a pose that is helpful to repeat because it brings the spine, legs, and arms into a neutral position. Downward Dog is an active, dynamic pose, but eventually you'll find it restful—even peaceful— as you advance your yoga practice. It just takes some practice and perseverence to develop your pose from a challenge to a reward. Try doing a few Downward Dogs early in class and then revisiting the pose at the end of the practice. You'll notice a big difference in how your body looks and feels in the pose.

Shoulder bones should slide down the back

downward dog

Feel the chest open as you press it forward

Spread the fingers and press evenly through each one

In Downward Dog, as soon as you get the feeling that you want to come out of the pose, its work is really beginning. To get the most out of the pose, you've got to persevere. Perseverance becomes very important in your teenage years. It's a life skill that can help you overcome hurdles to reach goals for yourself. Just like with the pose, it's helpful to establish a reference point for your goals—whether they include pressing your heels to the mat in Downward Dog or bringing up your biology average. Write your goals down and give yourself a time frame—it makes them easier to achieve and lets you appreciate how far you've come.

◁---- The hamstrings get a great stretch!

downward dog

You can transition into Downward Dog from standing poses or from your hands and knees. The palms reach forward, pressing into the mat. Try to spread your weight to every part of your hands as you lift the sit bones into the air. Press the heels toward the mat. The feet are slightly pigeon-toed, and the head looks through the arms toward the feet. If your legs feel uncomfortable, try bending the knees one by one until you walk out some of the tension. Feel your body relax deeper into the pose.

Press the heels down (but don't sweat it if they don't meet the mat) ◁---

*"Nothing great was ever achieved
without enthusiasm."*

*— Ralph Waldo Emerson,
American poet and essayist (1803–1882)*

confidence builders

Everyone gets anxious about trying a new sport or changing schools or making a new friend, but if you communicate confidence, everyone will rally behind you.

You become your thoughts: If you think you cannot draw, then you can't. If you tell yourself you can't run fast, if you put yourself down, those limitations will come true for you, too. Do you really want that? Girls are experts at putting themselves down. Recognize the power of your thoughts and turn them around! The best athletes are not always the fastest runners, but they believe in themselves, and they work hard. Let the strength you feel in yoga poses help you build that kind of confidence.

In the same way, you have to believe people want to be your friend. Don't assume that because they run with a different crowd they'll want nothing to do with you. Believe that you are unique and have so much to offer this world. Because you are, and you do.

fearless warriors

Live life confidently like a fearless warrior. Not arrogantly, but confidently. Sometimes just striking a pose of fearlessness can boost your confidence, as your body remembers its own power. Tap into that personal strength, and there is nothing you can't do. Another way to help yourself feel strong and confident is to focus on achieving something that's important to you. When you have a goal, looks and popularity don't matter so much. You realize that your destiny is in your hands. Your goals are in reach!

Life doesn't just happen. You make it happen; you create your own luck. It's not easy being a teenager, but sometimes if you just act like you know what you're doing, eventually everyone believes you do.

When you're feeling meek, try Warrior Poses to get yourself back on track. Hold each pose for several breaths, increasing the breaths each time. Let your confidence soar.

Straight, energized arms

Soften your gaze

Feel your spine come alive!

warrior sequence

Start with the legs far apart, then bend the left knee to balance in **Warrior 1**. Reach both arms up to the sky and sink deep into **Warrior 2**, opening the hips to the side wall. The arms open to both sides. For **Warrior 3**, soften your bent knee, then lift and lengthen the back leg while reaching the arms forward. Straighten both legs by consciously sending energy through the muscles and bones in your body. To modify, place your hands on your hips or extend them behind you.

Hips are squared to the front

warrior one

Back foot faces forward

warrior two

Reach the arms in a straight line

Vertical torso

Press into the outer edge of your back foot

be brave

If you've ever stood up for someone who was being bullied, you are a fearless warrior!

Both hips face the mat

Press evenly through the whole foot

Steeple grip

warrior three

Front knee is directly above front heel

from Mary Kaye's diary

One of my most fearless moments as a teen came out of one of my most embarrassing ones. I was a cheerleader for an important basketball game, but I had forgotten my bloomers. When my mom hadn't brought them by the start of the half-time rally, I decided to cheer anyway. When I jumped up the Velcro detached from my skirt and sent it sailing through the air. I stood there in string bikini underwear, frozen, in front of a thousand people. Then, I grabbed my skirt and ran out. I was hiding in a bathroom stall when several girls came in to laugh about what had happened. I decided I only had one option: stick a smile on my face and walk out with pride!

follow your own path

Follow your own path and discover who you really are. I believe we have different soul purposes during a lifetime, and I like to discover that purpose at each stage of my life. In your teen years, it may be focusing on academics. You may not even realize how important education is in these years, but knowledge creates confidence, so use that brain! However you define it, resolve to discover the meaning of life on your own terms. It's not what someone else has in mind for you. It's your path. Discover it joyfully!

Don't let past negative experiences define you or hold you back. Everyone has something that they aren't proud of. Everyone has a parent or friend that handled something less than perfectly. Forgive, forget, and move on. You define who you are, nobody else.

Don't sit back and watch life happen, either—jump in and see what you come out with! Warning: this is difficult to do if you're always watching TV, shopping at the mall, eating a lot of chips, or e-mailing your life away. Meet new friends face to face and discover what makes you tick. What's your purpose? It's up to you to discover it!

Focus straight ahead

Tuck the pelvis under

These legs can run!

crescent lunge

"Imagination will often carry us to worlds that never were. But without it, we go nowhere."

– Carl Sagan, astronomer (1934–1996)

popularity

One of the girls in my teen class said to me, "It's weird. We've moved a lot. At some schools, I am popular. Then I go to another school, and I'm not. Then I move again, and I'm popular again. Why is that?" Popularity is hard to define. Unfortunately, it usually has nothing to do with being a good person. It can change as fast as clothing styles. The only thing that matters is that you remain unaffected by it. Don't let being popular or unpopular define who you are. Just enjoy being you and remind yourself how much you have to offer this world.

Focus the drishti at the sky

Back leg is strong and extended

The arm acts as a lever to open the heart

These legs can dance!

crescent lunge twist

soul mates

Of all the relationships you'll have,

the one with your own body is the most important. As you get to know how the parts of your body work in yoga, you'll find some things in common with other relationships—your best friend, your dream boy, your cranky neighbor—you just need to learn to work through the challenges and find the goodness in each.

Being with a best friend or a boyfriend should be like being in yoga class: You can let your guard down, and it's truly OK to be yourself—with all your quirks and awkward moments. Failing in relationships and falling in yoga poses also have a lot in common: both bring you a step closer to getting it right. Don't beat yourself up when you say the wrong thing to dream boy or topple out of Triangle Pose. Just pick yourself up and try again.

Triangle and Half Moon Poses are challenging because your alignment goes in so many different directions; it takes balance to hold them together. Sometimes your life can go in a lot of different directions, too. Do you focus too much on a certain relationship? Let yoga open your mind to new people and hobbies. Reach out in these poses and in your life. And don't be afraid to fall—it's all part of building better balance, better friendships, and a better you.

triangle

Send energy up through the fingertips

Bump the hip back

Send energy down through the legs

patience

Do not sacrifice alignment by rushing into a pose. It's more important to lengthen the spine and feel the correct alignment than to make it into a pose but feel awkward. Take the time to check in with each part of your body. Listen to your breath. Use blocks often. And let go of your ego.

Active hands ----▷

Shoulders stack on top of each other

Flex the foot

half moon

Feeling steady? Try turning the gaze upward

from Mary Kaye's diary

When I was a teenager, I often wondered what falling in love felt like. When the quarter-back of our football team asked me out, I twirled in circles and fell down the stairs. I thought that I had found my soul mate! Like a fool, I squeezed into the tightest pants I could find, and couldn't walk or breathe the whole night on that first date. He was the first boy to tell me he loved me, and I thought he'd be the last. But after a while, he decided to date another girl, and I moved on. I felt sad but chose not to obsess over lost love and simply moved on for more adventure. Love happens, and it's wonderful. But it also happens again and again.

hip-hop hips

Active hands
send energy

Let your
joy show!

Revolve the
chest open

**side angle
stretch**

Knee lines up
above the heel

The hips store tons of emotion! When your feelings are hurt, you fail a test, or you can't seem to get out of bed, that sadness and tension get stuck in different parts of the body. One of the most common places to hold tension is in the hips, so releasing them can bring out incredibly strong emotions: you might feel euphoria, relief, or sadness—some people have been known to openly weep while holding hip openers. The release from hip openers is actually quite healing, so just let the emotions flow as you release negative feelings and make room for positive energy.

Here's one thing you can do with that new energy: Opening the hips with yoga makes dancing easier. If you love to dance, then learn how to loosen those hips! People who dance with tight hips look like they have to go to the bathroom. When your hips feel open and loose,

you can dance your heart out!
I always do yoga before I
go out dancing—it helps me
dance all night and come up
with some clever moves!
I feel more creative and
uninhibited when my body
feels flexible.

Feel totally hip!

Keep the
spine straight

Sink deep
into the hips

frog

Use the entire foot to
press into the mat

hip tips
spread kindness • dance
every dance • sing every chance • think
positively • laugh loudly • smile often
• help others • be your best • exhale
negativity • breathe

shine inside out

Real beauty shines from the inside out. Have you ever met someone you assumed was ordinary—then as you got to know her, she became one of the most beautiful people you ever knew? That's because beauty shines from the inside out. It's never really physical. It's a spiritual quality—an aura that surrounds people and makes others attracted to them. People who always see sunshine are far more attractive than those who focus on the clouds. The downers of the world are sick more than most, always complaining, blaming others, wondering why life isn't fair, or focused on what they don't like about a person or situation. Their obsession and negativity drains you. These people need to just let go, jump out there, and change their tune. (Don't tell them though, or they may attack the messenger—just hand them this book!)

Hip openers help you shine inside out. They release tension and nervous energy in the body. When you can release all the junk, you sparkle. You can't just sit around storing all that emotion. It has to go somewhere! You need options: yoga, a trusted friend, a journal, a dog to pet, a walk or hike. All these options help you unleash emotional baggage so you can go back to being you. All of us have baggage. We just need a few tips to help release negative emotion, so it doesn't start to affect our physical health, too.

one-legged dog

Press palms evenly
into the mat

Fully extend
the arms

Keep the leg energized!

Open up the hip

"*Sometimes your joy is the source of your smile, but sometimes your smile is the source of your joy.*"

–Thich Nhat Hahn,
Vietnamese monk (1926 –)

one-legged dog

From Downward Dog, reach one foot to the sky. Try to imagine touching a cloud. Really activate your feet. Now keep both palms equally pressed into the mat and open your hip by bending your lifted knee. Try to touch your foot to your head. (I don't expect it to happen, but that's the direction you want to open your body.) Don't forget to breathe in this hip opener!

Press the heel down toward the mat

open hips: open mind

Keeping an open mind opens doorways. It may seem easier sometimes to make snap judgments—but have you ever noticed how locking into one way of thinking can make it hard for you to see new opportunities? That's because when people try to define a person or experience, they're really setting limits about what they can expect of others and of themselves. When you decide that the new girl in school is not your type, you're telling yourself not to bother making friends with her. When you make a habit of laughing putdowns, like "I'm such a klutz!" you're saying to the world that you cannot be a beautiful dancer or a graceful yogi.

Yoga is all about being receptive to new possibilities. It takes some practice, but once you get the hang of keeping your mind and heart open, you'll start to see possibilities you never even considered. Hip openers can give your body the same feeling; settle into these challenging postures, and you'll feel like anything is possible! Bonus: When your body is open, it's easier to keep an open mind. Just as your body wants to discover powerful ways to move, your mind is hungry for knowledge and new experiences. Yoga challenges your body. It's up to you to feed your mind.

Lift up!

right on

When you do a pose that's not symmetrical, always lead with the right side of the body and then repeat on the left. Sometimes you'll notice one side is more difficult. In that case, repeat the pose on the more difficult side one more time to help improve flexibility where you need it most.

pigeon

Relax the hips as you fold forward

double pigeon

Stack the shins—first right over left, then left over right

bound pigeon

from Mary Kaye's diary

One evening in high school, a date was kissing me good night at my front door. Suddenly, my brother opened the door and screamed, "What happened to your face?" I ran inside to look in the mirror. There was blood everywhere! My date had had a nosebleed and had dripped all over me. The next day I found a note in my locker: "Sorry I bled on your face. Love, Dracula" I had been sure it was impossible to ever see him again—he would be too embarrassed, and so would I. But his clever note made me laugh and helped open my mind to date #2....

Revolve chest open

Release hip into the mat

"When you are content to be simply yourself and don't compare or compete, everybody will respect you."

—Lao Tzu, Chinese philosopher (7th Century BCE)

commanding respect

Command respect from your peers by thinking of others—help someone when they are lost, congratulate classmates on their successes, hold the door open for a stranger, or check to make sure a friend has a ride home. Kindness is contagious, and when people see you practicing it, they'll follow. Command respect by having the courage to open your heart.

Yoga prepares your body to sit up straight, open your arms, and smile. Sometimes these simple things are hard to do—especially if you are reserved. There's nothing wrong with being quiet. Shy people can be the best listeners in the world. They are also humble and easy to be around. But if your shyness keeps you from making friends easily or from interacting with others with kindness and confidence, then you are holding yourself back. Let yourself connect with others and show them what you have to offer. You command respect by being proud of who you are!

open your heart

When you open your heart, you uncover your true spirit and inner wisdom. How can you open your heart? Communicate candidly and honestly with friends. Remember that your family, your past, your personal style, your favorite music, and everything that makes you *you* is worth honoring. Don't hide away things that are important to you because you're worried about being judged. Opening your heart means making yourself vulnerable, but it also offers the rewards of truer friendships and the peace that only honesty can bring.

Remember that truly opening your heart is different from just opening your mouth to gab: It's not about spilling every little detail of your life or flirting like crazy. Guys are interested in flirtatious girls at first because it's easy for them. But the girls they really like are more into their own things, like yoga, drama, sports, or music. Work on yourself, and love will come.

A person with an open heart has such a natural, sympathetic way that she fits into any group. Heart-

from Mary Kaye's diary

In high school, my parents agreed to let me use the family Jeep if I promised not to let anyone else drive the car. But when one of my friends asked to borrow it, I was eager for her to think I was carefree so I handed her the keys. Later, the Jeep was totally trashed. When I saw the battered car being towed away, I broke down in tears. I realized then that honoring my agreement to take care of the car was way more important than trying to impress a friend by being reckless, but I'd been too scared to admit it. Open communication—even telling a friend they cannot borrow your stuff—helps you make smart decisions.

cobra

Keep the shoulders soft

Lift with your arms and abs

Keep the legs and feet together

camel

This is great for warming up to backbends!

Let the heels support your hands

opening poses let your body feel the same warm expansiveness your mind feels when it's open to new possibilities. You may feel vulnerable at first in a heart-opening pose, but after a while, the fear dissipates and you drop back effortlessly. Remember that feeling when you face challenges in your relationships. Your open heart can help bring peace to you and those lucky enough to be around you.

upward dog

Drop the shoulders down

Straighten the arms

The tops of the feet support your weight

Activate the thighs as they lift off the mat

Press evenly through your palms

compassion rocks

When you turn your focus inward, you can see your personality forming. Who are you becoming? Is it someone you would like to be friends with? As you start to accept and love who you are (and acknowledge where you could use some improvement), it becomes easier to really empathize with others and bring your compassion to the world.

Compassion begins with optimism. Do you see the glass as half full? Make it a habit to look for the best in others, and you'll be a strong source of support when your friends are down. You'll emanate rays of sunshine! Compassionate people are naturally appealing because of their sunny outlook. They find ways to help others because they themselves feel so fortunate. That's true compassion.

Are you more of a glass-half-empty kind of girl? Do you pity yourself when disappointed, or secretly rejoice when someone else experiences rejection? It is harder to feel compassion when you have a negative attitude. The good news is that you can

fish pose

This backbend feels amazing! Begin in a seated position with hands resting behind your bottom. Thumbs and forefingers should meet in a triangle shape. Extend the legs straight in front of you. Then lean back and rest your weight on your elbows, pressing your forearms into the floor. Arch your chest and lower the crown of your head to rest on the floor. Hold for five breaths.

bodhisattva

Bodhisattva is the state of altruism—finding joy through helping others. Go out of your way to help others without expecting anything in return. This is the secret to happiness.

Energize the legs

Point the toes

break the habit. Go on, ditch that little black cloud that's been following you around! Compassion heals your anger.

Personality is shaped by the way you approach life every day. You make the choice. Are you going to be compassionate? Yoga can help you refocus and see life in a different light. Let dynamic heart-opening poses help you learn to love yourself, forgive easily, and soak up the positive energy all around you.

from Mary Kaye's diary

In elementary school, I starred in a play as Eve opposite a boy who I had a huge crush on, who played Adam. As a souvenir, I took home a prop from the play—a huge rubber snake—and hid it under my mattress. One day when our housekeeper, Janie, moved my bed, the snake popped out. She raced out of the house screaming "snake!" A policeman heard her and rushed up to my room, where he drew his gun and shot the snake. When he realized that his victim was a toy, he was so embarrassed he begged us not to report the incident. My room was bullet-ridden and my secret treasure was destroyed. But I could see that Janie and the officer felt worse. I decided to overlook my problems. I saw that I had the power to choose my reaction and make them feel better. I also learned not to hide snakes in my room.

fish

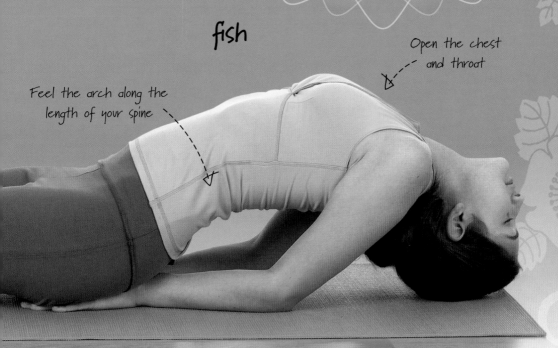

Feel the arch along the length of your spine

Open the chest and throat

bend over backward

Ever heard the expression "bending over backward"?

It's about someone who is flexible and giving enough to go out of her way—even head over heels—to help a friend. People at the receiving end of this kind of generosity have reason to be extremely grateful. Of course, sometimes you'll bend over backward for someone who doesn't deserve it—like a popular but rude boy or a "friend" who's only concerned with her own happiness. Just try to learn from these experiences so you can spend your energy better next time. Being a generous person isn't about giving away your stuff or becoming a pushover. It's about generosity of spirit—being willing to listen, spending your time with grandparents, sharing your company with someone who is alone.

I remember being tortured by my grandparents' lengthy discussion of lunch meats. I knew it was important to them to spend time with me, so I just smiled and acted interested. Now that my grandparents are gone, I'm really glad I spent that time listening. I know it brightened their day, and I actually learned more from them than I expected to.

Learn to stretch your body and open your soul, and when your help is needed, you'll be ready. Backbends give you more than an agile spine—they free your spirit and are energized expressions of joy! They also open the heart chakra, so generosity will come naturally.

Feel the front of the thighs lift toward the sky

Lift those hips

bridge

Fingers are interlaced

Feet are hip-width apart

bow

The arms are the string of the bow—straight and taut

Grasp the ankles from the outside

Look straight ahead and smile!

Keep the legs hip-width apart

This is great for the abs

Draw the belly in

counterposes

Remember when practicing backbends to do a counterpose after each sequence to balance the body. Try rocking into Dead Bug or simply hugging your knees to your chest. This gently massages the back and balances the stretch of a deep backbend. Hold the counterpose for the same number of breaths as you held the backbends.

While the body is energized, let the mind relax...

Inch the shoulderblades closer together to open the chest

advanced backbends

Stretching and moving the body help open up the areas that hold stress and sadness; flexibility is the state of being ready and able to bring about this type of release at any time. Keep the energy moving in your body, and you can let go of negative feelings more easily and always have room for optimism and strength. Backbends are a terrific way to do this; they release all the junk and negative emotions. Think of it as a cleansing process!

Backbends can make you feel like you are falling. Sometimes you feel vulnerable, a little helpless. But when you repeat several backbends,

wheel

Lift from the hips

Take five breaths

The back begins flat on the mat, then presses up high

Thighs rotate inward

Drop the head back ----⟶

Heart to the sky! ----⟶

Can you touch your head? ----⟶

king cobra

Keep the arms soft ----⟶

you overcome your fears and start feeling bolder and more joyful.

It's important to remind yourself that you are *not* helpless. Do you always have to watch your mom pick up your socks? Are you complaining that you can't find things before you even try to look? When you're thirsty, do you wonder how you will quench your thirst if you can't talk anyone into getting you a drink? If this sounds like you, find a way to do a backbend every day. Your feelings of helplessness are overtaking you, and you need to put on the brakes. Let your own strength and flexibility remind you that you are in control.

challenge yourself

Is there one pose you always want to avoid? That is probably the pose you should try more often. People often avoid a pose that focuses on an area of tension, when actually that pose would be a healthy release.

Try to overcome your fear; it will get easier over time. (If you're avoiding a pose due to injury, that's different—give damaged muscles time off before stretching them again.)

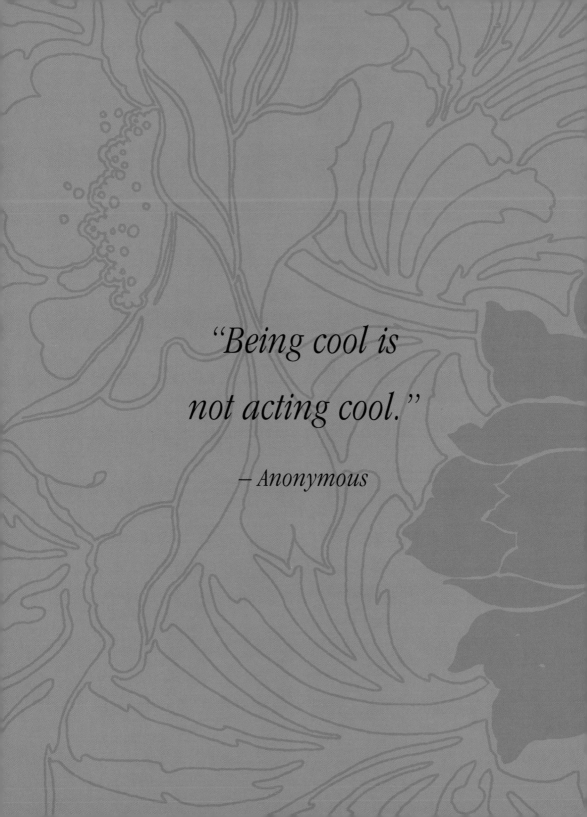

"Being cool is

not acting cool."

— *Anonymous*

cool to be me

Kindness is cool. So is being comfortable in your body. Lots of teens look at the outgoing, popular girl or boy as a model for what is cool. It might seem easier to dress and act in a way that follows their lead. Just be careful; imitating others can make you look just silly. And if you do it long enough, you may lose track of what made you different in the first place. As you develop your own character, you'll begin to recognize that it's that very difference that makes you cool. Don't let it slip away!

How can you nurture your cool? Be healthy. Respect your body by feeding it well and keeping it active. Keep your body moving to keep your mind clear of pettiness.

Avoid Gossip. Talking about other people screams insecurity. Feeling weak or fragile can tempt you to say unkind things about others. Hold onto your principles and resist.

Treat everyone as you wish to be treated. This is the golden rule of good karma. If you respect others and treat them kindly, great things will happen to you.

And, of course, always remember to breathe.

balance the body

Find balance in your life. Learn to gauge what you can fit in a day or week and let go of what you can't. By not overloading yourself, you leave room for peace of mind, which will help you release stress and self-consciousness.

A balanced body mirrors a balanced life. Standing poses test your body's balance, but also your mind's ability to stay focused and shut out distractions. When you master the ability to concentrate, it is easier to call on the strength of your body and your spirit; you'll be able to ignore negative or hurtful comments and let them roll off your back.

Before you try balance poses, try to slow down your breath by inhaling one long, deep breath and letting it all go on the exhale. Really feel your feet rooted into the mat. By allowing yourself to focus and balance your body weight on one spot, you begin the process of tuning out negative distractions. You will feel more centered and grounded. In each and every balance pose, try to bring back this awareness: rooted, balanced, breathing energy into each and every muscle. Let the balance in the body help you feel balance in the mind. This is an opportunity to get focused and be present, to generate confidence and even out emotions, to focus on you and the coolness of what your body can do.

blind balance

To make balance poses even more challenging, try closing your eyes. Always focus on becoming perfectly still before adding in a new level of difficulty and testing your mind's ability further.

"Stand up as yourself. Do not imitate. Do not pretend to have achieved your goal, and do not try to cut corners. Just try to grow."

– Swami Prajnanpad, yoga master (1891-1974)

Press the hands together if you can—
or just bring the left hand as far as you
can and grab the right forearm

Keep the gaze straight ahead,
into and through the arms

eagle

Eagle Pose is a deep, twisty stretch for the
upper back and shoulders. Begin in Mountain
Pose and find your drishti (focus or gaze)
directly in front of you. Connect with the mat
with your left foot. Take your right leg up and
over the standing left leg and wrap it around.
Now take your right arm under the left arm
and wrap it until your palms connect (or as
close as you can get them). Lift the arms so
that the elbows are shoulder height. Try to
sit into the pose. Rise out of the pose slowly,
then try it on the other side.

eagle

Wrap the foot around
as far as you can

Ungrip the toes

balance your life

Get organized. You can't have a clear head if you can't see the floor of your room, so make time to get rid of the clutter. Keep what is absolutely necessary and donate or toss all the little knick-knacks you've collected for so long. This cathartic practice will leave your head and your room feeling a lot lighter. When you're surrounded by clutter, your mind gets cluttered. When your environment is clear and organized, you'll be amazed at the mental energy it frees up.

Once you clear the clutter in that brain, use it! Enjoy a good book. Research a story for the school newspaper. Pick up a paintbrush, if that's what moves you, or play around on your guitar. Find your passion. You've created this peaceful space—it's yours to enjoy.

Just as you clear your physical space, clear the distractions around you in balance poses. Focus on your drishti and carefully tune out all other distractions. Ignore the other yogis as they wobble, and the traffic passing by, and any other distraction in your environment or your mind. Balance is creating stillness and peace amidst chaos.

Reach out with electricity!

Focus the drishti (gaze) between your hands

lightning bolt

Squat as though you are sitting in a chair

Keep your knees together

Clasp the ankle and lift!

Look straight ahead, over your arm

dancer's pose

loosen up

Sometimes when a tough pose draws a lot of attention to one thing—like not falling over—it's easy to let other parts of your body tense up. Remind yourself to relax the shoulders. Lengthen the neck. Ungrip the toes. Unclench the teeth. Soften your face.

Keep the arms active to help you balance

Both hips face the mat

Focus on the edge of the mat

airplane

tricky arm balances

It's great to be confident—but watch out for the overly confident teen. You've got to find the right balance between acknowledging your strengths in a healthy way and announcing them to the world. Let's say you are very smart and get 100% on most tests. Most likely, your classmates know that academics come easily for you, but they will come to resent it if you insist on sharing your scores every time. Learn to be humble about your successes. The talented athlete achieves satisfaction from playing well and making the score. It is never wise to rub it in the losing team's face or to gloat about your achievements. Remain humble and let your peers talk about your successes. They'll be even more impressed that you can take it all in stride.

Lift the navel
to the spine

crow

The knees balance
high on the back
of the arm

be your best

A true yogi is focused inwardly when practicing yoga and doesn't waste energy comparing herself to those around her. I remind my students that there may always be someone smarter, stronger, more athletic, more flexible, prettier, or richer than they are—but no one has to be kinder. You control that!

I remember hearing a beautiful girl announce to her peers that all the boys liked her. What do you think all the girls did? They talked behind her back...constantly. Confidence is good. Overconfidence is obnoxious.

These arm balances are tough—you've got to approach them with humility and respect—but that doesn't mean you shouldn't try them with faith in your own ability to learn. Whenever I demonstrate a tricky pose, all the teens in my class immediately chant, "No way!" Their minds quickly try to shut them down: "I can't do that...it's too hard...the yoga teacher is crazy." In the end, though, they all get into the pose.

Lift the gaze so you don't go splat!

side crow

Center your weight so you can balance on the arm

more tricky stuff

These tricky poses help you recognize your own power. Take control of your fear and act with confidence, and you can handle tricky poses—and tricky relationships, too. How do you know if you're in the wrong relationship? When there's a lot of flash in front of his peers and false promises, and then when he's with you, there seems to be little interest unless he's kissing you. When is it time to dump him? It's time to move on when he lies, hurts you emotionally or physically, questions what you wear, how you look or who you hang out with, or puts you down in any way. Sometimes it's hard to see a relationship for what it really is when you're in the middle of it. Realize that if you don't both bring out the best in each other, it's probably not meant to be.

When you feel in control, you have the confidence and clarity to understand when you need to get out of unhealthy relationships. Power poses help give you the strength to make a change. So what if your first impression about him was wrong? People make mistakes like that all the time—

firefly

⊀---- Cool dreadlocks

Yogi toes ---- ⊀
are active

⊀---
When you center
your body weight,
you feel weightless

crow/firefly

---- Balance on the highest point of the arm

it's just part of the process of figuring out what you do and don't want in your relationships, and it's an easy fix.

Power poses demand a lot of energy, so they're a great opportunity to build strength and appreciate your body. They also take courage. Take this time to look inside yourself, test your own boundaries, and take pride in your successes. Be your own cheerleader! Once you take control, you'll have the confidence to hold onto power poses and get out of bad relationships. Be bold.

from Mary Kaye's diary

I dated someone who I thought was the love of my life. I was impressed with the surface—his looks, athletic ability, his crazy dance moves—all the wrong things. Over time, he became competitive and jealous. He started questioning everything I did. My body started to show symptoms of stress. My back broke out in acne for the first and only time in my life. Then, my best friend demanded to know why I didn't just dump him. At first, I was offended, but then I started paying attention. I got out, and the acne left.

"The best way to cheer yourself up is to try to cheer somebody else."

Mark Twain, American author (1835-1910)

powerful posture

People decide how they feel about you in the first ten seconds of meeting you. That's why the way you walk, sit, and hold yourself determines how people respond to you. It may not seem fair, but it's just human nature that the first impression is the strongest.

Yoga continually encourages the lifting of the heart, softening of the shoulders, and lengthening of the spine—in other words, simply beautiful posture. This kind of stance not only makes you look better; it also communicates a very definite message to those around you. Think about it: People who dismiss good posture and flop over might as well mutter "don't bother getting to know me." Good posture says, "I am confident and self-assured. I am interesting. You'd be crazy about me!" It tells others that you like who you are. That's a powerful message to send when meeting new people or entering new situations. (And every day is a new situation!) So walk with grace. You'll like where it takes you.

tummy toners

Core strength makes perfect posture. When your core, or ab section, is strong, you carry yourself with attitude and grace. Toned abs make it naturally easier to maintain a straight back at the dinner table, prance around in high heels, and lug around your bookbag—not to mention look fabulous in a swimsuit! Be charming and graceful, using your abs to hold your head high and walk with poise. Toned abs also give you a healthy dose of confidence.

Having a strong core in your teenage years will help you later in life, too. A toned tummy keeps your back straight and improves your posture. It also helps you in yoga twists. You can do all the crunches you want, but there's nothing like yoga for core strengthening.

There are several simple poses that help promote good posture. Plank Pose and Boat Pose are two of the most effective poses in strengthening and lengthening the spine and creating a strong core. They're also two of the most challenging poses for many women. Help out your abs by activating the legs and sending energy through every muscle and bone. Imagine the muscles hugging the bone. Tummy toners are active poses, so feel the energy move!

breathe
Breathe into your full body in every pose. Let the breath connect you to your body, head to toe.

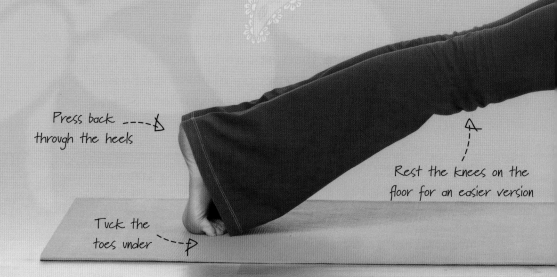

Press back ----▷ through the heels

Rest the knees on the floor for an easier version

Tuck the toes under ----▷

Roll shoulders
back

Lift the heart

Active feet

boat

Bend the knees for
an easier version

Balance on the
sit bones

Focus on the
front of the mat

Pull navel to spine

plank

tone and twist

Sit up tall ---

Even when life gets all twisted, you should still be able to breathe. Remain calm in a bind—that is life's great test. Sometimes you have a day that just doesn't make sense. I had a morning where I woke up, watched my dog poop out my favorite fuschia leather glove, zapped myself walking through his electric fence holding his collar, then drove him to the park in two different shoes because I couldn't find a match, only to have him open the sunroof with his head, dumping two feet of snow into the car...and that was just the first 20 minutes!

In life and in yoga, when you are in a crazy position, you should still be able to breathe. In fact, you should be able to laugh!

seated twist

Twists cleanse the body of toxins, and they tone abs. They also massage the internal organs and leave you feeling invigorated. I find twists really relaxing, too.

To really benefit from toning and twisting, consciously pull the navel to your spine on the inhale and sit up tall. Deepen your twist on the exhale. Remember to breathe and actively send energy down through your spine and out through your limbs. Breathe through the whole body.

--- Revolve the
      chest open

∮----- Deepen the twist
          on the exhale

from
Mary Kaye's diary

One time I got twisted. It wasn't really planned that way. (It never is.) I entered into my high school talent show with a group of friends. I was cast as the Good Fat Fairy for the skit, and my friends really wanted me stuffed with pillows and in roller skates. I was back stage waiting to go on, but I missed my cue. My dear friend Ann gave me a good ole push in the rear end and launched me off the stage, sending me sailing on roller skates, wings flying, airborne in straddle split, head on into the judge's panel. (That was my first straddle split.) Somehow we still managed to get second place, but I couldn't walk for a week. To avoid getting twisted in life, don't just do what your friends tell you to do. Rely on your own strength and smarts to guide you.

seated twist pose

While seated on your sit bones (the bones of your bottom), bend the right knee, letting it rest on your mat. Take your left foot and place it outside and to the right of your right leg. Make a comfortable seat but keep the sit bones grounded on the mat. On the inhale, lengthen the spine. On the exhale, twist. Repeat this on the other side to balance the body.

stand tall

Balance poses help you stand up straight

so you don't slouch or stick out your bottom. (Not that your bottom isn't adorable.) Remember, strangers and friends alike will respond to your body language, smile, and manners. Just like your tone of voice says more than your words, crossed arms, a hunched back, and rolling eyes all send messages. Body language is an important way of communicating with your peers— some experts even say that it's more important than the words you choose.

The simple act of crossing your arms sends the message "stand back." Slouching over says "don't notice me." These are closed messages. You may not even be aware that you're sending them because it's become habit. By uncrossing your arms and sitting up straight, you'll send a more positive and open message to people. Look people in the eye. Answer questions with an engaged response. Be curious about others.

Relax the shoulders

Palms press gently

Foot presses on the inner thigh (or below the knee for an easier version)

Knee opens the hip

tree

"We first make our habits and then our habits make us."

– John Dryden, English poet (1631–1700)

Yoga can redefine your posture. By training your body to stand in a positive, welcoming way, your yoga practice can transform the message you send to the world. If you don't want to say, "stand back," consciously practice heart-opening poses that force you to open your arms. Stand tall, and make a habit of pulling your navel to your spine—that one simple but effective yoga concept can transform every pose. As you stand tall and steady, your ears should be over your shoulders, shoulders over your hips. Keep this vertical line straight. Practice, practice, practice…so it becomes habit.

Unclench the teeth

Active arms remain beside the ears

leaning mountain pose

body talk

Most of us are not conscious of the messages we send through body language. Try videotaping yourself with a friend—do an interview or skit—and you'll notice how you carry yourself. What message do you send? Are you open or closed?

Rotate the thighs inward

strong, steady, and bold

Today, we are bombarded with technology, quick fixes, and ways to become disconnected to a personal experience. Ever notice how much more confident and fearless teens come across via IM or e-mail? Then you meet them face to face, and it's like a totally different person. There's danger in relying on computers to build connections with people. You lose so much—expression, tone, attitude, humor. Some people even get so caught up in their IM life that returning messages is like a full-time job. Try to sneak away from the computer world by being strong, steady, and bold in your real relationships. Computers can be a crutch that don't allow you to fully experience being—you're really having a relationship with your computer, not a person. Sure, computers are great for academics and research, but not to truly get to know someone. Are you brave enough to embrace the real world and all the possibilities it holds?

Try these energetic poses to help you be strong, steady, and bold on your mat. Rely only on your own strength and purpose to tune out distractions and hold the pose. When you are able to focus your drishti on a point and block out interruptions and sounds, you can focus your mind on any goal, any relationship, any test. With the world becoming increasingly materialistic with so many choices and temptations, being able to focus and shut out the noise is a gift. When you are strong in your ability to focus and in your convictions, you are unstoppable.

Elbows hug the body

Lift the heart

chaturanga

Hands in reverse prayer
or hold opposite elbows
for an easier version

feet first

For all standing poses,
press the four corners of each
foot evenly into the mat and lift the
arches of your feet. Lift your kneecaps to
engage the muscles. Let your body connect
with the mat, then find your drishti. Are
you gripping the mat with your toes?
Relax the feet. Think happy feet.

pyramid

Lead with the heart
as you fold over

Both feet
are grounded

Knees lift (or drop knees to
the mat for an easier version)

"*Remember when,*
'you play like a girl,'
use to be an insult?"

— Mia Hamm,
American Olympic soccer star (1972–)

athleticism

Whether they're sprinters, sluggers, or slam-dunkers, athletes already know the benefits of an active lifestyle. People who do sports are stronger, have more endurance, and stay healthier than couch-potatoes. But what these sporty chicks might not realize is that practicing yoga can multiply those benefits and help them see results they could never achieve with one form of fitness alone.

Sports tighten and build bulk in muscles; yoga lengthens and strengthens the muscles. It changes the look of your body by stretching the muscles long and lean. The toning benefits also enhance performance and flexibility; with yoga, athletes can actually train their bodies to avoid sprains and strains, or bounce back quickly if they are injured.

Yoga complements many sports, and sporty types love that it's a creative way to build muscle tone. It's also a great change of pace for people who are used to zipping around the track at top speed. So don't let making varsity label you as a jock—roll out a mat and get twisty. Yoga is for everybody!

inversions

Life can make you feel like you're turned upside down. But actually, that's a great place to be sometimes. Inversions let the blood and energy flow "up," toward your heart and brain. Blood flow to the brain can wake you up and stimulate the mind. Inversions energize—and they can also help you look at the world in a whole new way. Sometimes viewing the world upside down allows you to find the humor in difficult situations. I have noticed that people who can find a good laugh in a bad situation bounce back more quickly than those who dwell on the negative.

Some of the girls in my classes love inversions so much they want to jump right into them at the beginning of every class. I know how they feel—being able to hold your body in such an unusual posture makes me feel like I can do anything! But I like to save upside-down poses until everyone's body is warmed up and ready for the challenge. Remember to treat your body with care. Flip upside down and discover a brighter outlook on life.

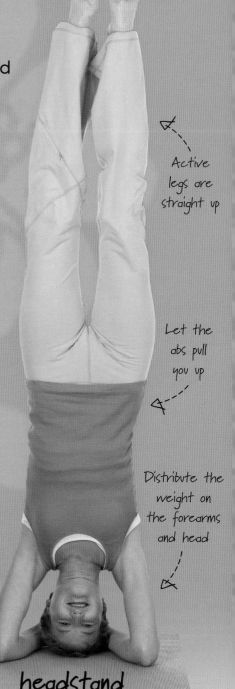

Active legs are straight up

Let the abs pull you up

Distribute the weight on the forearms and head

headstand

from Mary Kaye's diary

When I was younger, my dad would ask us who could stand on their heads the longest. I knew it was a trick to get us to stop bickering, but my brother, sister, and I would drop what we were doing and pop right into headstands. Then, Dad would walk out of the room and leave us there standing on our heads. It worked every time.

find the humor

Headstands and handstands are crazy inversions.
I like to walk on my hands and turn out
the lights with my toes; it just
creates a change of pace
and makes me laugh.

tripod

&---- Tuck tightly

&---- Build a strong base

&---- Head and hands form
the points of a triangle

love life upside down!

As with anything new in life, the more inversions you do, the more comfortable you'll be with them. Soon you'll be able to try new positions, such as Shoulder Stand and Plow Pose. You'll find a way to love life upside down just as much as right side up! When you're in these poses, take your time to appreciate a new point of view. We're always on our feet, so your body will appreciate another perspective.

These poses are totally satisfying when you master them; they're a test of your yoga prowess and a gift for your heart and mind, all at once. This is where all that work on your abs and your balance pays off. The trick to flipping safely into an inversion is to start with a good connection to the ground and to your core. You'll use the strength of your abs, or core, to lift up and over and keep your body steady. Let your shoulders bear your weight and support your neck while your abs help you move and steady your body.

Remember to ease into these positions slowly, leading with your legs, then count five full breaths while your body rests in the pose. You can do it—just take your time, think positively, trust your body, and roll with it.

Reach toes to the sky

Straight active legs

Balance on the shoulders not the neck

Always support the back

shoulder stand

*Blessed are they who can
laugh at themselves,
for they shall never cease
to be amused.*

-Anonymous

healthy
mind

Athletic people are use to
physical skills coming easily for
them. Yoga may not. Competitive
people who excel at sports may
struggle with yoga poses.
They might also find it
tough to break the
habit of trying
to outperform
everyone in the
room. Yoga is not
a contest. It's not
a sport. It's humbling.

Draw your belly in ----▷

Lift the knees
and straighten
the legs

plow

stretch the shoulders

Your shoulders influence the way you walk—and the way you feel. Walking with slumped shoulders not only looks bad, it actually has a negative effect on your emotions. The next time you feel yourself slouched over, try to notice if you feel tired or down. The way you walk with your body affects how you feel, and the way you feel shows in the way you hold your body. When you're happy, you lift your chest and roll the shoulders back. Try to mimic that posture when you're feeling blue and see if you can lift your spirits just by lifting your posture. Your shoulders play a critical roll in your well being—don't neglect them!

For athletes, fluid upper body movement is critical for success on the court or on the field. Tension in the shoulders can lead to headaches, a stiff neck, and a limited range of motion. Tight shoulders affect your tennis serve and golf swing. Heavier backpacks can also take a toll on shoulders. It's important to do gentle shoulder rolls so the shoulder blades lift up and slide down your back. You can even do this sitting at your desk.

Make time every day to stretch out those shoulders. Try starting your day by flopping over in a forward fold. That's one of the simplest and best shoulder stretches you can do. You'll feel your body wake up as the blood rushes to your face, the chest opens, the shoulders release, and the spirits lift.

dolphin

cowface

mind over matter

Go into yoga poses
without any expectations.
When you expect a pose
to be too difficult, it is.
When you go without any
expectations, you'll be
amazed at how much
you can do!

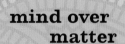

Clasp the
hands or
both ends
of a strap

Knees
stack
in front

Relax the neck

Press the chest
toward the mat

Arms are parallel
to each other

let's split

Just the mention of the word "split" can make people want to jump out of their pants. Do not be afraid of splits. People tend to avoid events, sports, situations, and people that look challenging or like too much work. You miss so many great opportunities if you close your mind to challenges. All you have to do is try these deep stretches while taking slow, long rhythmic breaths. Each day will be a little different depending on how you feel, but it is always worth trying something you may not think is possible. No one expects you to be perfect.

Of all the poses, splits probably require the most patience and time easing in and out. Take life and your yoga practice slowly, savoring the moments, noticing the feelings, enjoying the laughter, being present. Your breath can help you slow down, so take the time to regroup and focus on inhaling and exhaling. It reduces stress when you learn to breathe through challenging poses without letting them frustrate you.

Hips are even ---- ▷

straddle split

Outer edges of the feet press into the mat

Drishti is at the floor

from
Mary Kaye's diary

I really wanted to split during one airplane trip.
I had just gulped down two huge bottles of water,
and between me and the bathroom was a stranger in
the aisle seat, who was fast asleep, drool running down
his face. I was ready to wet my pants, but couldn't wake
him. I thought I could test my yoga skills and do Frog Pose
or a Straddle Split over him. Time was running out. So I
cautiously stepped one leg out to the aisle. Several rows
of people looked on. Pressure was building. Finally,
I lifted my leg ever so gently to escape. The man
jumped. I screamed! We collapsed on top of
each other. The onlookers went wild. He
smiled and said he thought he
was in a dream.

straddle split

From Mountain Pose, jump your legs
out to straddle position. Slowly, with the
breath, bend forward at the waist and
sink deeper into the pose. The outer edges
of the feet should press into the mat. You
can stay balanced on your palms or, if you
can go deeper, rest your weight on your
elbows and forearms. You don't need to go
all the way down. Getting there is a slow
process that requires lots of patience!

running wild

Nothing is quite as powerful and exciting as watching wild horses running wild through open space....or a dynamo teen striding down the field to take a shot on goal! Although you can't try it on a horse, Runner's Lunge is a beautiful stretch that prepares the body for running wild down that turf field. Athletes particularly love the way Runner's Lunge makes them feel, but it's a great stretch for anyone at any time. It reminds you of the power of your legs and your body. Every chance you get, you should run wild. Run wild through an open meadow, the beach, or a snowy field. Enjoying the little moments makes life seem simpler. Running in your neighborhood is also a great way to take in the seasons and become familiar with your community. Live passionately: Get out! Breathe! And remember, you are powerful, fast, explosive!

Running feels great because it's wild and free—but start right by making the time to prepare your body and stretch

from Mary Kaye's diary

One Fourth of July, I decided to really make an entrance to the water. I started running, racing really, over the crowded beach and toward the water and did a round-off/back handspring and dunked under the crashing waves. When I stood up to wave my brother and his friends into the water, they didn't respond. I thought they couldn't see me so I jumped up and down and screamed louder, "Get in, chickens!" Finally, he yelled back: "If you pull your top up from around your waist, maybe we will!" It turned out that I was the firecracker show that day!

This is the best for tight ----▷ hamstrings!

Press back into the heel

Leg is straight and strong

your muscles after running. Strength is beautiful in girls—both mental and physical. Take time to take pride in that strength and care for your muscles. Stretch them long and lean. There's no stopping you now.

Lengthen the spine

Knee lines up over the heel

runner's lunge

runner's lunge

Step one leg forward in a giant lunge. The knee should line up directly above the heel. Your strong, straight back leg balances on the ball of the back foot. Come up on your fingertips, lifting the chest, and hold the pose for five breaths. Roll the shoulder blades down the back. Then switch legs. To modify, place your hands on blocks instead of the mat.

Come up on the fingertips

"Life is not about finding yourself.

Life is about creating yourself."

– George Bernard Shaw,
Irish playwright (1856–1950)

creativity

Try to live more in your heart than in your head, and creativity will come to you. It stifles creativity when you tell yourself, "I can't do it." Teenage girls are especially guilty of putting themselves down or talking themselves out of trying something new or different. I still shake and shiver when I hear a girl in my class declare "I can't do Crow!" Everyone I have ever met in yoga class has the ability to do some version of Crow.

Your mind has the power to shape what you can and cannot do; it is not your body that limits you. Stop telling yourself that you can't write or draw, especially if you enjoy it. If it's hard for you to think positively, then avoid people who put others down. Maybe you don't even realize that you're surrounded by downers. Listen to what your friends are saying so you can recognize and tune out negative messages. Then, listen to your own heart and mind. Only you can determine who you become.

partner poses

Create supportive bonds by practicing yoga with a partner. Take this chance to reach out to someone new or someone you might not know very well. It doesn't mean you are forever connected to him or her. It's like a dance—just try it out and see whether you work well together. Working well with others is a skill that you can develop; every time you reach out to help others, you get better at it. This skill helps you get team school projects done better and faster, snag a decent summer job, or play a key role on the student council. Your partner poses are an opportunity to reach out and make a team effort. Partner poses allow you to move your muscles in a stretch that is longer, deeper, and more comfortable than holding some yoga poses on your own. Plus, the partner who is supporting the pose

Count out five slow breaths

wheel assist

Support the back

Clasp ankles securely

trust

Keep in mind while you're having fun that you're also responsible for taking care of your partner. Don't jerk her around or drop her in an effort to be funny. Earn her trust with your support.

can offer guidance on form. They might say, "draw your shoulders down" or "relax your jaw." It's ideal to find a partner of your same size, but if that doesn't work, any friendly face will do. Just find someone who enjoys yoga as much as you and get started.

Treat each other with respect, approaching each pose gently. But don't let things get too serious—working with a partner is a great chance to lighten up and laugh. There's one teen in my classes that doesn't love touching other people's feet in certain poses. She has some sort of odd foot aversion. So of course, I always touch her feet. This sends everyone into fits of laughter. Laughter lifts everyone's spirits.

Straight back

Hold onto wrists

cobra assist

Hips press into mat ----▷

why not?

Why not more partner poses? Partner poses are a great way of meeting new people and learning to trust. You should assume that everyone finds you interesting. Sometimes shy girls assume the worst: that they have nothing interesting to say or that people would prefer to be with someone else. Trash that negative thinking! It's simply not true.

If you get anything out of your yoga practice, let it be the ability to break your mind of negative thought patterns. Don't be hard on yourself for thinking these thoughts—they happen to more people than you can imagine. Even the supposedly confident teen feels self-doubt. Don't let negative thoughts make you hide away; try reaching out to a friend, instead.

The power of touch goes a long way. Even a small gesture like a pat on the back or a squeeze of the hand shows support and kindness. Sometimes teens avoid this kind of contact, but as long as it's done in a respectful way, it can be positively comforting. It just shows you care. It's not weird.

So, grab a partner and get started with some more twisty fun! And give someone a hug or two.

seated partner twist

Cross your arms and grab hands

Press your backs together to help elongate the spine

"An acquaintance that begins with a compliment is sure to develop into a real friendship."

— Oscar Wilde, Irish poet and playwright (1854–1900)

spread love

I always give prizes out in yoga. If someone learns a new pose or does a backbend after telling me that they will never do a backbend, I like to give a prize. They always get excited to win the prize until they find out what it is: a hug. But you know what? Now, they look forward to my prize.

Legs are together and active

Keep the back neutral

supported headstand

Distribute weight evenly between head and palms

go with the flow

Get closer to your mat to wind down, relax the body, and calm the mind. Now that you have flipped, split, stretched, bent, and lifted, it's time to spend some time on your booty. Being relaxed and laid back makes people feel comfortable. When people feel rushed or stand in long lines, they tend to get agitated. Only you can overcome that kind of stress by changing your breathing and changing your mind. If you're typically wired and high energy, identify things that help relax you and find ways to be more casual. Maybe you notice that you're calmer at the beach or with a certain friend. You'll be easier to be around if you aren't always talking and trying to outdo everyone. Just breathe.

If, on the other hand, you're already so relaxed it takes a crane to get you out of bed, find ways to energize yourself. Maybe you need to enter a writing contest, take up a photography course, or get a job. Discover what interests seem to motivate you to do more.

just be

Let go of ideas of perfection. Yoga is not going to make you perfect. When you spend so much time trying to be perfect, the message is "I'm not okay as I am."
Be as you are.
Revel in it.

one-legged forward bend

Lengthen the torso over your extended leg

Hook onto the feet

Foot presses on inner thigh

rock the baby

Cradle the shin to the chest ----⋉

That's what I love about yoga—it can relax you, but it's also energizing.

As you start to slow down at the end of class, your joints will feel different than they did when you started. Releasing your hips should be much easier now, so you can try a beginner seated pose and then take it to new levels. As you advance your practice, you'll be able to move from a simple seated pose such as Rock the Baby to a more advanced arm balance such as Elephant Pose. When you feel ready, experiment and see what your body can do. It may surprise you!

elephant

Tip the body ----⋉
forward

Send energy through the legs to lift the body. You can do it!
⋉

Center your body weight

Hook the ankles

make your own poses

As a child, I invented, with pride I might add: high heeled socks, a contraption to knock my sister out when she came to steal my angora sweater, and a funnel at the dinner table that released under the table and fed my food to our dog. Dare to be different and think outside of the box—no matter how outlandish your ideas may be. Find an idea you like (like ditching your broccoli under the table) and take it one step further. In your yoga practice, try to take your poses one step further each time you practice. Maybe that means holding yoga poses longer or asking a new person to be your partner or trying to stand on your head. Whatever you find challenging, test yourself little by little.

Walk the legs up the wall to a right angle

Feet press against the wall

Straighten the arms to build strength

"Take everything you like seriously, except yourselves."

– Rudyard Kipling, British author (1865–1936)

downward dog on a wall

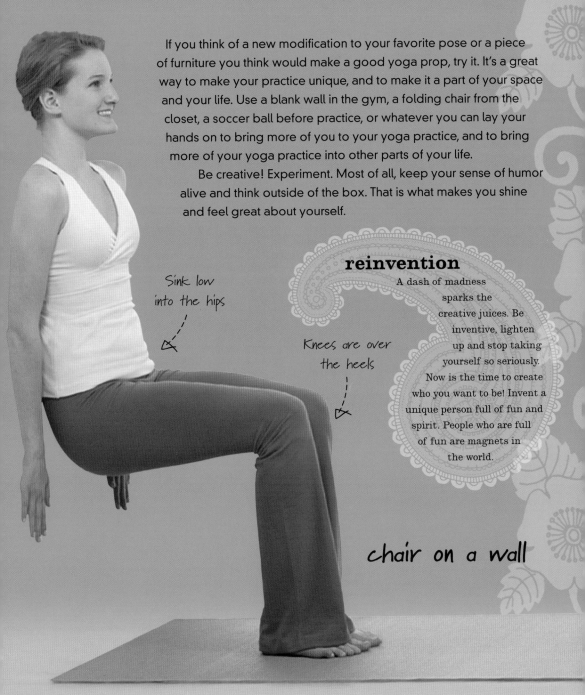

If you think of a new modification to your favorite pose or a piece of furniture you think would make a good yoga prop, try it. It's a great way to make your practice unique, and to make it a part of your space and your life. Use a blank wall in the gym, a folding chair from the closet, a soccer ball before practice, or whatever you can lay your hands on to bring more of you to your yoga practice, and to bring more of your yoga practice into other parts of your life.

Be creative! Experiment. Most of all, keep your sense of humor alive and think outside of the box. That is what makes you shine and feel great about yourself.

Sink low into the hips

Knees are over the heels

reinvention

A dash of madness sparks the creative juices. Be inventive, lighten up and stop taking yourself so seriously. Now is the time to create who you want to be! Invent a unique person full of fun and spirit. People who are full of fun are magnets in the world.

chair on a wall

"*Be who you are and say what you feel, because those who mind don't matter and those who matter don't mind.*"

– Dr. Seuss,
American children's author (1904–1991)

what's right for your body

Treat your body with respect. When you are proud of your body and respect who you are, you can consciously develop good habits to improve your overall well-being. Even if you have bad habits, it's never too late to reinvent yourself! Find ways to sweat, get sleep, avoid soft drinks, drugs, and alcohol, drink more water, dance your heart out, laugh with friends, enjoy hobbies, and breathe. As you take care of your body, you'll have pride in its shape and the awesome power it holds.

Remember to listen to the messages your body is sending you, and take care of it. Whether you're yawning for some extra sleep at night or realizing that you'd feel more comfortable in a modified pose, it's up to you to treat your body right. Even when it seems like life is racing by, it's worth the time and effort to take care of yourself and give your body what it needs. Feed your body, respect your body, pamper your body. Take care of your shell. Don't let it crack.

all about props

If your body isn't quite ready to go deep into a pose, there are lots of yoga props designed to let you keep proper form without going all the way. You can find blocks, straps, blankets, and bolsters at most yoga studios. But if you don't have the official prop you need, don't sweat it: A phone book or folded blanket can work just as well as a block, and a tie or belt can make a perfect strap. Raid your dad's closet to find what you need. As long as it helps you go deeper into a pose or a state of relaxation (and your family members don't mind the loan), it's a good yoga prop. Props are great for helping maintain good form, but don't become so preoccupied with the props and getting the alignment right that you lose the moment. Be in the moment.

Don't be embarassed about using props; learning to modify a pose to suit your range of motion is a sign that you're in touch with your body and working with it in a responsible way. Some poses, such as forward bends or standing twists, can be deceptively tricky. If you're in one and find yourself wishing for longer arms, grab a prop. You'll get the most out of a pose if you're comfortable and relaxed. Don't try to do more than you can.

seated forward bend

Straps help pull the navel to the thighs more easily

laugh test

Don't force yourself into poses. You should always strive for your individual edge, but not by muscling into unnaturally deep stretches. Alignment is way more important than looking like the teacher. You know your body. If you cannot breathe comfortably in a pose, it is too difficult for you—let go of your ego and reach for the block or strap! You should be able to breathe, smile, laugh!

Let the added height help align the shoulders

Bend from the hip joint

triangle

Legs are three or four feet apart

"Some people move our souls to dance."

— *Anonymous*

if you're overweight

Weight is a major preoccupation in the teen years. (When I was a teen, I could polish off a plate of brownies in five minutes flat—and it showed!) The constant media attention to tiny celebrities and skinny models only exacerbates the fear that your body is less than perfect. When you feel frustrated with your weight, remind yourself what you love about being you!

If you're overweight, some yoga poses can feel difficult or just uncomfortable. There are lots of ways to modify poses to make more room for the belly. You can widen the legs in folded positions or find ways to distribute your weight when your ankles or wrists feel strained.

from
Mary Kaye's diary

In my late teen years, I gained lots of weight. Yes, I was fat. It was painful being ignored when I was heavy. People don't mean to be hurtful, but they treat heavy people differently. No one really made much effort to get to know me. Yoga helps me maintain a healthier weight now, but people still make a double-take when they see pictures of me from the chunky days. I always had a smile on my face, but I was hurting inside. It was so hard to lose weight—nobody realized how hard I was trying. I wish I had known about yoga then. It would have helped me deal with the pain. Now I know not to judge others by the way they look. Fat chicks rock!

Hold the body straight and strong

modified plank

Let the knees share the weight with your wrists

Relax the neck ---- ▷

Knees are a few
inches apart `--▷`

table

▷ ---- Lift the
hips high!

Over time, building arm
strength also helps you lift your
weight and hold poses more
easily. Keep practicing the poses
that challenge your arms. (But if
you're overweight by 30 pounds
or more, avoid inversions.)

Yoga will help you shed
pounds if you also control
your portion sizes. Never
obsess over your weight
or exercise—just try to
make smarter choices and
don't give up if you fall
out of line once in a while.
Everything in moderation.

get fit

Want to drop some pounds?
Drink lots of water, limit
your portion sizes, and eat
a healthy breakfast. Make
time every day to burn
some calories—whether it's
soccer practice, yoga class,
or just a long walk around
the neighborhood. Your
body will thank you!

**modified
pigeon**

Both hands
hold the thigh

Balance on
the sit bones

if you're not flexible

Not everyone was born flexible, and everyone learns at a different rate. Some people need a little more time and patience to feel confident in different poses. What's easy for one person feels completely different to another person. Don't let that stop you—every pose has easier versions so that everyone can find a way into it. Some people are stronger than they are flexible. The idea is to find a balance so you are as flexible as you are strong.

I was a gymnast as a teen, so yoga was easier for me as an adult than for some of my friends, but that doesn't make me a better yogi. There are poses that I am still working on and seem far, far away. I don't fret about it because just getting there is part of the fun! Some days you feel tight—you just need to take it slower until your body is ready to loosen up.

If your muscles feel tense, don't push to straighten your legs all the way or outdo the twist you did last week. Try bending then straightening one leg at a time to walk out some of the tension. Keep your knees soft when you need to. You don't need to tie yourself into a pretzel to get full benefits from yoga.

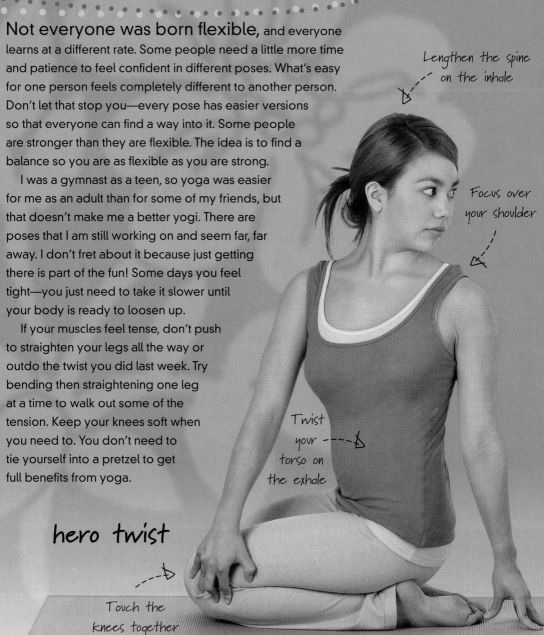

Lengthen the spine on the inhale

Focus over your shoulder

Twist your torso on the exhale

hero twist

Touch the knees together

sphinx

Relax the shoulders away from the ears

Soften the face

Actively extend the legs

Mini-backbend

it's about you

There's a misconception that you need to be flexible to enjoy yoga. Yoga isn't about being super-bendy; it's about improving flexibility and connecting with your body. Don't worry if you can't plop into a split. Push negative emotions like envy out of your mind. It doesn't matter if Susie can put her leg behind her ear. Let your body call the shots.

modified runner's lunge

Extend the arms

Press the hips forward

if you have a headache

Got a headache? Don't skip yoga! Now is when you need it most. With some modifications to make things easier on your aching noggin, some yoga poses can do a world of good for a mild headache. For more severe aches, get yourself into a dark space and relax in Savasana.

Headaches are caused by the swelling and constriction of blood vessels in the face. They can be triggered by hormonal changes, stress, weather changes, diet, sleep, dehydration, car sickness, skipping meals, and some medications. Most likely, the stress of your day is stuck in your head and neck. You can get unstuck by trying a sequence of forward bends to release the shoulders down the back and let go of tension. Try these poses when you start to feel stress, and you may find your headaches becoming less frequent and less severe.

Any pose that allows the blood to release to the head improves blood circulation and alleviates headaches. Try Child's Pose with your forehead resting on a block. Downward

Lengthen the torso

Legs are engaged ----▷

standing forward bend

Release the head completely

child's pose

Hands reach forward
or rest by your sides

Calm
the mind

Lay torso between
the thighs

Big toes
touch

Dog, Dolphin, Standing Forward Bend, and Rag Doll are excellent
inversions to ward off headaches. And if it's stress that aggravates your
head, try Savasana with a lavender eye pillow. Sometimes darkness over
the eyes and soothing smells alleviate the pain. Try not to focus on the
pain—think about what makes you happy. Take your practice slowly and
let your body heal itself with some help from you. Drink lots of water.
Eat regular meals. Try to avoid stressful situations or relationships.
There are solutions.

chill out

Sometimes when my
daughter has too much going on, she complains of a
headache. She'll drink a lot of water and then heat
up a lavender eye pillow in the microwave to place
on her eyes. She likes essential oils rubbed on her
neck and feet. She creates a virtual health
spa in her bedroom! It always helps her.
Try to discover what your body
wants when it's aching.

if you have back problems

Stress, weight, poor posture, and sports injuries are all common culprits in cases of back pain. Back pain can make you lose your focus. But doing yoga can help build awareness and poise to help prevent future aches and pains and relieve the ones you already have. Poses that work your core are great for supporting and strengthening the back. You'll also benefit from meditating in an upright, seated position that keeps your back aligned.

Do you have a strong back? If you feel the small of your back and it has a little ditch down your spine, you probably do. But you may struggle in backbends because your arms or back muscles need strengthening. Determine what poses make your back feel great and do them often. Keep

cow

Move the gaze up slowly

Drop the belly

Round the back

Press the heels back

cat

Drop the gaze toward the navel

an eye on your posture, too; standing up straight helps strengthen your back while you're just walking around.

Another condition that can make it more challenging to stand tall is Scoliosis. Scoliosis is a slight curvature of the spine that many girls develop in their preteen and teen years. If you've been diagnosed, talk to your doctor about using yoga as part of your physical therapy.

If your back is aching, avoid deep backbends like Wheel that could intensify back pain. Instead, try Cat and Cow poses whenever the class is doing a backbend. They're great for soothing and strengthening. Try modifying other tough poses by dropping your elbows or knees when you need to. Send love to that back!

grow

Girls skyrocket in growth during the teen years. You may find that you tower over all the boys. Did you know that you actually draw more attention to your height when you slump over? It just looks odd, so people wonder what is wrong. Even if your boyfriend fits in the crook of your armpit, there's no need to act like a hunchback. Standing up tall says "This is who I am!"

Navel pulls to spine

Lift the thighs

dolphin plank

if you like to take it easy

When I was a teen we played a specific sport only during the designated season. At my school, soccer was played in the fall, then lacrosse in the spring. Times change quickly. Now kids play multiple sports all year round in addition to spending time on musical instruments, hobbies, and homework. This makes it even more important to take the time to stretch and rest to protect that active body! It's easy to get wired from all the activity, but it's important to get your schedule down to a manageable level. People who have less time have less patience. I worry about people who are afraid to go slow and take it easy. Are you running all the time? Remind yourself that there's a huge difference between mindfully taking it slow and being lazy. You need to be kind to your body and give it the rest it deserves.

Make a list of what you need to do in a week. Is it overwhelming? How does it make you feel? If you are struggling with doing all of it well, then you probably need to cut back on something. Talk to your parents and explain that even though all your friends play soccer (or take ballet or edit the school newspaper), you don't love it

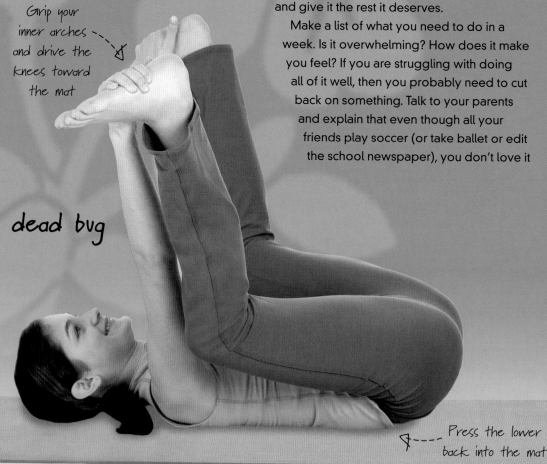

Grip your inner arches and drive the knees toward the mat

dead bug

Press the lower back into the mat

Drishti focuses over
the opposite arm

reclining
knee twist

Both
shoulders
press into
the mat

Knees press
together

and would rather put that energy into
something you like better.

It took yoga to make me realize
that not only is it OK to slow down, it's
necessary for good mental health.

Head hangs heavy

*"You will do foolish
things, but do them
with enthusiasm."*

– Colette, French novelist
(1873–1954)

rag doll

Hold opposite hand
to opposite elbow

Move weight into
the balls of the feet

"When your body is tranquil,
you will know bliss.
Because you are blissful,
your mind will concentrate easily.
Being concentrated, you will see
things as they really are.
In so seeing, you will become aware
that life is a miracle."

– Buddha, in Digha Nikaya, a collection of discourses

savasana

Savasana is a time to clean the slate and settle into a quiet, clear state of mind. Erase all your mistakes, stop feeling guilty, and forgive yourself for putting your foot in your mouth. So what if you thought her mole was a piece of brownie stuck above her lip. She's probably heard it before, so you can just let go. As you let go, you'll feel a wave of relief. A calm peacefulness plants in your heart and will last as long as you want it to. You're no longer holding a pose. You don't have a worry in the world.

Savasana is the ten to fifteen minutes of your practice when you lie still and clear your mind of chatter. Prepare your mind for meditation. Savasana is also the Sanskrit name for Corpse Pose, which looks like the easiest thing in the world, but is a very challenging pose because it's about emptying all the worries, all the thoughts from your body and mind. Some people don't really get the purpose of just lying on their mat, and others say it's their favorite part of yoga. Whatever it is for you, it's still important that you make time to go deeper into your heart and a state of relaxation. There is a beautiful person inside!

restful poses

As you prepare for Savasana, find a place you love that is peaceful, happy, and quiet so that you can wind down with restful poses. Use these restful poses as gentle ways to slow down your practice so that you can mentally prepare for Savasana.

Your environment is critical for your solitude, happiness, and yoga practice. Ever notice how people who live in warm, sunny places are super friendly? There's a reason for all the good cheer. You can create your own sunshine—a cozy environment for your mind at home or in Savasana. When the yogi next to you is full of chatter, try to shut her out by feeling compassion for her. She's still struggling with learning how to create stillness in her head.

As you rest, let go of any anger that prevents you from being happy. Release negativity. Find the humor in embarrassing situations. And enjoy being in your own body—nobody else is quite like you, and that's extraordinary.

inner calm

As your body rests, visualize a bright white light soaring down into the crown of your head and spreading slowly throughout the body. Let it envelop you and bring you peace.

yoga mudra

Take hold of one wrist

Keep those sit bones grounded

Rest the forehead on the mat or a block

modified happy baby

Hug knees to chest

Gently hold outer edges of feet

Soften the face

Take Savasana to a deep state of relaxation by releasing your jaw, softening your eyelids, unclenching your teeth, softening your cheeks, closing your eyes. Let negative feelings drain from your body, and allow your body to melt into the mat. You'll begin to feel light, like you're floating. When you've challenged yourself with yoga postures, you deserve a peaceful reward in a restful state. Discover what you appreciate about being still. Stillness helps you grow.

"Among those whom I like or admire, I can find no common denominator, but among those I love, I can: all of them make me laugh."

-W.H. Auden, American poet (1907–1973)

why and how to meditate

When you meditate, you let your mind listen to the messages of your inner voice. You may become inspired and suddenly realize just what you need to do next in your life. But your mind must be clear of all thought to begin the process and allow meditation to reveal your purpose.

Meditation is the experience of clearing your mind of mental chatter. Even if worrisome thoughts do intrude on your peaceful state, you'll be able to react to them differently. They have less control over you as you begin to have a deeper understanding of self.

Soften the gaze

Release the shoulders

easy pose

Free your mind of negative thoughts and feelings of sadness, jealousy, anger, pity, and regret. Let go of draining thoughts, or anything you might worry about but cannot control. Let only positive thoughts stay in your mind; let them encourage peace, creativity, love, and happiness.

The end of your yoga practice, when your body is exhausted, is an ideal opportunity to meditate. But you can meditate almost anywhere—the beach, your room, by a stream. All you need is a quiet space.

Samadhi

Someone in a state of Samadhi is perfectly awake and alert but has gone beyond the boundaries of unconsciousness. It's a feeling of complete joy and peace. Samadhi is the absolute final goal of meditation; it is oneness with the universe and with God.

easy pose

Sit tall and straight in a relaxed cross-legged position. Hands rest on the knees or press together in prayer position. Close your eyes if you want to. Take your time to inhale, then exhale, and slow down your heart rate. Clear your mind. Purge all negative thoughts.

"You must learn to be still in the midst of activity, and vibrantly alive in repose."

– Indira Gandhi,
former Prime Minister of India (1917–1984)

meditation prompts

Meditation nourishes the heart and clears the mind. It's an amazing tool—but it might take some time and practice to master it.

Many people find it difficult to be still. Some people are so busy in the rest of their lives that it feels unnatural not to be using every minute to work or plan or think or get ahead. Some just like to hear themselves talk. Savasana is the most challenging part of a yoga class because we can always think of something that needs to be done or said. When I first began to relax in Savasana, it felt impossible. I wanted to jump up and dance. It was hard to sit still. That's when I realized that I needed Savasana more than most people. It's even more important for active, high energy people who like to go, go, go!

This meditative state should be considered your reward for practicing yoga. You worked hard to earn it, so take it seriously. It's not cool to fidget. But it's also not cool to judge people who do fidget. They'll get there. If you have trouble keeping your focus, ask your teacher for some meditation prompts or techniques to bring your mind back. Don't give up. It takes practice to really enjoy it, but over time you will love the way you feel after fully releasing all your thoughts. Now I like to take Savasana several times during my practice. Some people mistakenly think they can do yoga without the critical practice of Savasana, but it is this part of yoga that creates a peacefulness within you that stays in your heart and keeps you coming back for more.

"Meditation is to be aware of every thought and of every feeling, never to say it is right or wrong, but just to watch it and move with it."

– Krishnamurti, yogi and philosopher (1895–1986)

lotus pose

Feet press into ----▷
opposite hip creases

Straighten
the back

meditation prompts

Color Imaging: Think of your favorite color. Let this color surround you. Try to fully experience it as you breathe. Now, breathe through all the colors, picturing each vividly as you go: Think, "Breathe in red, breathe out red. Breathe in orange, breathe out orange." Continue through the rainbow.

Loving Meditation: This meditation brings love and kindness to your heart. Begin by repeating. "May I be fearless. May I be kind. May I be happy. May I be peaceful." Repeat quietly in your head. Invent your own phrases.

Nature Prompts: Imagine a favorite place—maybe the ocean and its rhythmic waves crashing at the shore. Feel the sand and smell the salty air. Let yourself drift away from the material world and toward a state of nature.

Sounds of Life: Practice slowing down the breath and bringing awareness to the sounds around you. As you sit quietly, you'll start to notice an entire new layer of other sounds. Listen for sounds on top of sounds. Layers upon layers.

be happy

Now is the time to just relax and feel joy. You have reached for goals and achieved them; take time to appreciate all your hard work and talent. Let go of expectations, enjoy quiet and solitude. Let your inner happiness glow.

Happy people make others feel good. They send positive energy into a room. Happy people don't expect material things or other people to keep them smiling. They understand that everyone is responsible for creating joy in her own heart. Happy people like to dance and sing! And you won't hear a happy person saying, "I'm bored." They recognize that they are the only one that can fix that problem. They bring out the best in everyone because they focus on the positive.

be real

Money, good looks, and status symbols cannot make anyone happy. Material things will never make people like you (no matter how hard you buy). How you treat others is ultimately what attracts real friends and brings happiness.

Corpse Pose is the ultimate pose of blissful relaxation. Get comfortable and lie back. Let your palms unfold and your feet flop open. Fold a bolster, blanket, or mat under your knees, if it feels good. You can also drape a blanket over your body. The weight and scent of a lavender-filled eye pillow can help relax the mind and soothe the

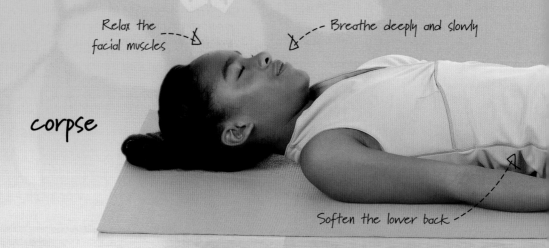

Relax the facial muscles

Breathe deeply and slowly

corpse

Soften the lower back

corpse with props

An eye pillow can help you block out distractions

A pillow or blanket under the knees feels great!

eyes. Tense all your muscles and then release them. Watch thoughts drift by in your mind. Do not judge them or analyze or wonder. Just watch them float and notice how intent your mind becomes on distracting you. Each thought goes on a tangent. Just watch and take notice. Let go.

Savasana should last at least ten minutes at the end of your practice—but the exact amount of time isn't important. Once you stop fidgeting, you are in Savasana. Empty your mind of any chatter. Be still. Just breathe.

from Mary Kaye's diary

One of my teen yogis confided in me about a sad weekend: She had been invited to a slumber party, but was then told that the sleepover part had been cancelled. It seemed odd, but she happily went to the party thinking the hostess had just changed her mind. The truth was that all the other guests were still sleeping over—only she had been uninvited. When one of the other girls let the secret slip, she was deeply hurt. It didn't make sense; she had done nothing to deserve it. Sometimes jealousy or just a bad mood makes people behave in cruel ways. Don't try to analyze the logic when there is none. All you can do is try to release the hurt and let go.

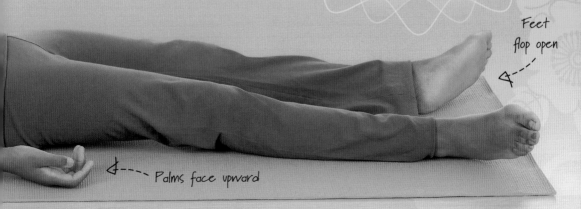

Feet flop open

Palms face upward

"*Never, never give up...*

unless you get really tired.

-Ellen Degeneres, American comedian(1958-)

practices

As you become more familiar with yoga poses, you can link them into a series, breathing from one pose to another in a fluid sequence. Using the poses together is the best way to get yourself energized in the morning or to mellow out before finals; you can fine tune your practice according to how you feel any given day. It can also just be fun—it's like following a choreographed dance.

Remember to make every pose an active pose, and enjoy discovering your favorite transitions. I love moving from Warrior Two into Half Moon Pose. It flows naturally and sets me up to balance, making me feel centered and strong. I also like to flow from Eagle Pose into Airplane. It helps me determine how balanced I feel that day and where I may get stuck. You can twist for energy or fold for calmness. Making transitions from one pose to another helps you become more graceful and dynamic in the poses. At first you'll bump along, but then your practice will evolve into a flowing meditation.

sun salutations

Sun Salutations can actually reverse depression by waking up your body and releasing emotional imbalances. They start the day out right. It's an energizing flow of linking the breath to dynamic postures. You'll combine balancing poses with forward and back bending poses. You must be in a mindful state, practicing with the breath, and repeat Sun Salutations to get full benefits.

1. Stand tall in Mountain Pose. (p. 13)

2. Lean forward in Swan Dive.

3. Gently fold into Standing Forward Bend. (p. 104)

4. Lift your heart to lengthen the spine. (p. 148)

5. Jump or step back into Plank. (p. 67)

6. Lower body in Chaturanga, tucking arms to the side. (pp. 72-73)

7. Roll over the toes and lift into Upward Dog (p. 47)

8. Roll back over the toes and press into Downward Dog. (p. 28)

9. Look forward, bend the knees, and jump forward on the exhale.

10. Slowly rise from the hips and center the body in Mountain Pose. (p.13)

wake-up call

Just when your alarm goes off and you slowly creep out of bed, find comfort knowing it's the perfect time to practice Wake-Up Call. This practice is for people who dread getting out of bed. It's designed to activate the senses and pump you up with renewed energy. It's simply a great way to start your day so you're mentally alert and prepared for all the surprises to come!

1. Sit up tall in Hero Pose and twist to both sides. (p. 102)

2. Drop back and open your heart in Camel Pose. (p. 47)

3. Melt into Child's Pose. (p. 105)

4. Lift up and arch back in Camel. (p. 47)

> *"Respect for ourselves guides our morals;*
> *respect for others guides our manners."*
>
> – *Laurence Sterne, Anglo-Irish writer and clergyman (1713-1768)*

5. Round the back in Cat Pose. (p. 106)

6. Arch the back in Cow Pose. (p. 106)

7. Roll the feet over and press up into Downward Dog. (p. 28)

8. Sink into the breath and release your chest in Child's Pose. (p. 105)

energize

If your energy is low, your feet are dragging, and you just can't seem to do anything right, try jumping back in your day again with Energize. This dynamic sequence of poses is also helpful if you need a second wind for the night because you're going out dancing. It moves the body in a fluid, graceful dance and opens your hips, too. You'll feel rejuvenated and ready to embrace the world! Energize moves the body in strong, challenging poses. To get the most out of this practice, hold each pose for several breaths each.

1. Stand tall in Mountain Pose. (p.13)

2. Step back into Warrior One. (p. 32)

3. Open your hips to the side in Warrior Two. (p. 33)

4. Stretch the torso up and over in Reverse Warrior. (p. 146)

5. Straighten the front leg and grasp the front ankle in Triangle Pose. (p. 36)

6. Bend the front knee and ease into Side Angle Pose. (p. 38)

7. Lift up to balance in Warrior Two. (p. 33)

8. Balance in Half Moon Pose. (p. 37)

9. Ease the back leg down and bend the front knee into Warrior Two. (p. 33)

10. Press the palms at your heart in Mountain Pose. (p. 13)

Repeat the entire sequence on your other side.

stress relief

This practice is for when you just can't take much more.
The Pop Quiz was not what you had in mind...toilet paper dragged from behind
your skirt and your crush waited until the end of class to alert you...even your dog
forgot to greet you when you came home. But that's all behind you now. Time
to clean the slate and start over. You need solitude and a peaceful space. Even
though your day was less than ideal you won't rehash. You're moving on. Stress
Relief offers poses that relax the senses, release stress, and move the body in
gentle stretches. Think sunshine!

1. Sit on the heels and sink into the hips
   in Child's Pose. (p. 105)

2. Interlace the hands and roll onto the
   crown of the head in Rabbit Pose.

3. Release back into Child's Pose. (p. 105)

4. Lift the heart to rest on your forearms
   in Sphinx Pose. (p. 103)

5. Inhale up into Cobra, then rest and repeat this pose. (p. 48)

6. Release to the forearms and roll the shoulders back in Sphinx Pose. (p. 103)

7. Walk the feet in lifting the sit bones in Dolphin Pose. (pp. 80-81)

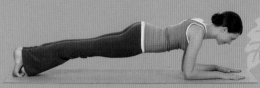

8. Walk the feet back and engage the abs in Dolphin Plank. (p. 107)

9. Release onto the mat, then lift your heart and legs in Bow Pose. (p. 51)

10. Push back into Child's Pose (p. 105)

bendy back

When you feel tight all over or need a pick me up, try the Bendy Back Practice to discover renewed energy. Backbends are energizing and full of happiness. As you lift the body in Camel and Wheel, feel a smile in your chest. You'll positively feel better and strengthen your back muscles in the process. Joy starts in the heart radiating out—backbends lift the heart and help you radiate all day. Find joy, then spread it everywhere!

1. Round your back in Cat Pose. (p. 106)

2. Let the belly drop as the hips and head lift up in Cow Pose. (p. 106)

3. Rise on your knees and arch back clasping the heels in Camel. (p. 47)

4. Fold into Child's Pose. (p. 105)

5. Clasp your hands, then lift the hips and inch the shoulders together in Bridge. (pp. 50-51)

6. Lift up into Wheel. (p. 52) (Repeat.)

"The control center of your life is your attitude."

– anonymous

7. Now enjoy a counterpose, Dead Bug. (p. 108)

8. Hug the knees to the chest.

9. Rock up into Shoulder Stand and support your back. (p. 78)

10. Roll back into Plow. (p. 79)

11. Lie flat, then arch onto the top of your head in Fish Pose. (pp. 48-49)

12. Relax in Corpse Pose. (pp. 118-119)

balance your nerves

Got the lead in the play? Nervous about the big game? Can't seem to get the butterflies out of your tummy when you pass your crush? You are the ideal candidate for Balance Your Nerves. When your nerves are shot, you need to find comfort and calm energy. Take the time to stand in Mountain Pose and repeat positive mantras: "I am peaceful. I am confident. I am a strong athlete. I am." You can talk yourself into a peaceful state. Never forget the power of the mind! Balance Your Nerves helps you learn how to go with the flow and not feel so rattled.

1. Stand tall in Mountain Pose. (p. 13)

2. Step into Warrior One. (p. 32)

3. Open up into Warrior Two. (p. 33)

4. Wrap your arms and legs in Eagle. (p. 57)

5. Extend your leg and arms behind you in Airplane. (p. 59)

6. Pull in your raised leg and press it to your inner thigh in Tree. (p. 70)

7. Lower to the mat and cross leg over the resting knee in Seated Twist. (p. 69)

8. Lift the body straight and strong in Plank Pose. (pp. 66-67)

9. Press back into Downward Dog. (p. 28)

10. Melt into Child's Pose. (p. 105)

Repeat sequence on opposite side.

power yoga

Power Yoga appeals to athletes and teens who like to push it to the edge. You are probably the type who plays attack in sports. You have high energy and thrive in competitive situations. You have a hard time winding down at night because you race all day. You do everything fast—talk fast, walk fast, study fast. Power Yoga is your speed! Just make sure you find time to practice peaceful, soothing poses as well.

1. Energize the body in Downward Dog. (p. 28)

2. Roll the feet under in Upward Dog. (p. 47)

3. Press back into Downward Dog. (p. 28)

4. Jump the feet to the front of the mat.

5. Press the knees out in Seated Prayer. (p. 24)

6. Lift the body in Crow. (p. 60)

7. Step onto the mat and then jump the feet back.

8. Steady the body in Plank Pose. (p. 67)

9. Lower down into Chatarunga. (p. 72)

10. Flip the feet and press into Upward Dog. (p. 47)

11. Hold Downward Dog for five breaths. (p. 28)

total confidence

Uncertain? Shy? Speechless? Total Confidence helps you believe you can do anything! Conquer your fears, and life just gets easier. Trying poses that make you fearful and mastering them is the first step towards conquering your fears and gaining more confidence. You should also practice trying one thing that scares you every day. Give yourself an extra little push! Do these empowering poses on your right side first, then your left.

1. Lift from the crown of the head in Mountain Pose. (p. 13)

2. Lift the heart while folding forward over the front knee in Pyramid Pose. (p. 73)

3. Lift the back leg and find your balance in Warrior Three Pose. (p. 33)

4. Turn the feet and knees out in a deep squat for Frog Pose. (p. 39)

"I do not try to dance better than anyone else. I only try to dance better than myself."

– Mikhail Baryshnikov, Russian dancer (1948-)

5. Sink low into Straddle Split. (pp. 82-83)

6. Lift from the core into Headstand. (p. 76)

7. Take the feet then the knees to the mat into restful Child's Pose. (p. 105)

8. Try to balance your body weight on your arms for Side Crow. (p. 61)

Repeat the entire sequence on your other side.

yoga booty

Everyone loves a yoga butt. They don't shake as much as others do, and they're pert, round, and noticeable. Take your butt into your own hands with Yoga Booty. Do not hide your butt. Be proud—bottoms are important tools. They take the blow when you fall. They take dance routines to a whole new level. They allow you to rest, meditate, and just sit. They can also help you balance in seated poses like Boat. Try Yoga Booty and be proud of that caboose!

1. Stand tall in Mountain Pose. (p. 13)

2. Point the toes out and sink low into the hips in Frog Pose. (p. 39)

3. Step feet together in Mountain Pose. (p. 13)

4. Sit back low into the heels and reach up in Lightning Bolt. (p. 58)

5. Roll back in a tight ball and lift back up to standing.

6. Energize the thighs and sink back into Lightning Bolt. (p. 58)

7. Reach one leg back and press arms forward to balance in Warrior Three. (p. 33)

8. Bring the feet together and roll back in a ball to massage the spine.

9. Balance on your seat and lift the legs and arms up in Boat Pose. (p. 67)

10. Lie back, then press up into Bridge Pose. (pp. 50-51)

Repeat the entire sequence, doing Warrior Three on your other side.

bedtime yoga

Winding down to go to bed can be a challenge. Do you find ways to put off bedtime? If so, try Bedtime Yoga about one hour before you want to go to sleep to help you relax and sleep better. There's no sense in making yourself look awful the next day by pushing your body to hang in there every night. Find ways to manage your time better so that you're not exhausted. It's hard to have fun when you're pooped!

1. Take hold of the inner arches and press the knees downward in Dead Bug. (p. 108)

2. Release the feet and slowly lower the legs to rest in Corpse Pose. (pp. 118-119)

3. Gently hug the knees to the chest.

4. Roll back and forth in a ball, massaging the back.

*"The pessimist sees difficulty in every opportunity.
The optimist sees the opportunity in every difficulty"*

— *Winston Churchill, former British Prime Minister (1874-1965)*

6. Lift the legs up and over your head, and contract the abs in Plow Pose. (p. 79)

5. Lying on the back, drop the knees to one side in a Spinal Knee Twist. (p. 109) Repeat on the other side.

7. Lie flat, then lift up on the elbows and drop the head back in Fish Pose. (pp. 48-49)

8. Lower the body to melt into the mat in Corpse Pose. (pp. 118-119)

"Think about what yoga can do for you. Then find your passion, spread kindness and laughter, and most of all breathe. Only then will your soul start to dance."

— Mary Kaye Chryssicas (1965-)

your yoga journal

Express yourself. Your yoga practice is an outlet that will help you learn to love who you are, and make it easier to speak your mind.

In your life you'll almost certainly meet people who are better artists or can belt out a song on key or are more confident. Sometimes that can shut you down—you start wondering how you stack up. Recognize that talent takes practice. It takes enthusiasm. It also involves finding the thing you love and really going for it. This isn't easy—it opens you up to criticism. But guess what? The critics are usually the ones sitting on the couch, not caring about anything but the next opportunity to talk about someone. Don't listen to negative messages; find your passion and be yourself.

Finding your passion makes it easier to be yourself. Worrying about what other people think only slows you down. When you move your body in unusual ways in yoga poses, you start to feel more comfortable putting yourself out there—and literally sticking your butt in the air. Now that's freedom! Move that booty and take pride in your accomplishments!

what's your style?

Which style of yoga is right for you—your personality and body type? Take this yoga quiz to assess your learning style:

1. **What do you really expect from a yoga class?**

   a. It should be a great workout — I want to have sweat dripping off my body and feel sore for days.
   b. I like hard work but am most interested in alignment and how each pose should feel exactly.
   c. I just like to relax with gentle stretches and then pass out.
   d. I want to meditate about my boyfriend while finger painting his picture.

2. **Which bedroom do you identify with most?**

   a. A canopy bed and homework all over your desk, scrapbooks, photographs, tennis racket, maybe a softball glove on the floor.
   b. A modern bed with everything in the right place. Homework done and in a neat pile. Books lined up. Color coded wardrobe.
   c. Sweet bunny bed with your dog curled up at the end. Your own paintings all over the walls. Poetry, letters, and inspirational phrases stuck all around.
   d. Hammock tied to two palm trees, preferably with a monkey.

3. **For fun, which would you prefer to do?**

   a. Rally a game of football or tennis or find some friends to go hiking—anything active!
   b. Organize my music collection, take a walk, read a great book, play with my dog, or go shopping.
   c. Find a beautiful spot in nature to just sit and think.
   d. I'd wear a wig and walk around town getting to know people.

4. **How would you act in a yoga class?**

   a. I would fly in late after my tournament, beg to borrow a mat, and kick off a conversation with the nearest yogi.
   b. I would arrive early, line up my mat, blocks, and props neatly before me, and make small talk until class started.
   c. I would arrive on time and melt into Child's Pose or a deep meditative state to mentally prepare me for the class ahead.
   d. I would bring in my hedgehog, sit him on my mat, and hide until the yoga teacher noticed it wasn't me.

5. When you were younger, your favorite activities were:

a. riding a minibike, scaling the tallest tree, or waterskiing.

b. doing ballet, twirling a baton, playing ball, or collecting rocks.

c. writing poetry, keeping a journal, or helping my mother bake.

d. dancing in my underwear in front of the mirror, squirting ants with Gatorade, or shooting your sister's feet with your BB gun to make her dance.

6. Your ideal date is:

a. backpacking up a mountain in a bikini and hiking boots.

b. a pleasant dinner date at an ethnic restaurant, then head out to a fun party or movie.

c. picnic under a weeping willow tree by the lake with a canoe set up for a romantic ride.

d. head to a football stadium in full body paint to see the Patriots, your favorite team, then wrestle the mascot to the ground while your date comes in to save you.

ANSWERS:

If you circled mostly As, you will love Ashtanga and Bikram yoga. If most of your answers are Bs, Iyengar could be the style for you. If you answered C to most of the questions, check out Kundalini and Kripalu. And if you circled Ds, you are nuts, and I'd like to party with you. But keep in mind, while this quiz will find the yoga style that's most like you, it's also wise to try your opposite style for balance. Be open minded and try new classes when you find them. Namaste.

HATHA: This is a yoga style that focuses on both poses and yoga flow for strengthening, opening, and cleansing the body. Hatha is the most popular form of yoga and teaches that the body is a vehicle of the spirit. Iyengar and Ashtanga are forms of Hatha.

ASHTANGA: Ashtanga, or power yoga, is a challenging workout that moves through a series of poses with ujjayi breathing. It is a dynamic flow that requires strength, stamina, and flexibility. Ashtanga is best for people who already have some yoga experience.

BIKRAM: Bikram Yoga studios are heated to 100 degrees to help yogis go deeper into poses and sweat out toxins. A class performs 26 poses twice. Bikram always stretches muscles in a specific order: standing poses, backbends, forward bends, twists.

IYENGAR: Iyengar Yoga focuses on precise details and perfect alignment in the poses. Poses are held longer and repeated. Iyengar makes frequent use of props like blocks, blankets, and belts. The layout of the studio is unique, too: two rows of mats face each other.

KRIPALU: This yoga style helps connect the breath with body and spirit. There are three stages: 1) learning the poses and breathing; 2) holding poses and increasing awareness of thoughts and feelings; and 3) meditating as you flow from one pose to the next.

KUNDALINI: Kundalini Yoga was brought to the West in the 1960s. It focuses on the release of Kundalini energy (serpent power) which is located at the base of your spine. Kundalini Yoga focuses primarily on chanting, breathing, and meditation for spiritual transformation.

what's your dosha?

Ayurvedic Yoga is an ancient healing system from India.
Ayurveda, which means "the science of long life," relies on natural methods of healing, such as food, herbs, yoga, and meditation. Ayurveda is based on the theory that people have dominant traits in certain doshas. You can actually identify your dosha, Vata, Pitta, or Kapha, by understanding your physical, mental, and emotional attributes. Doshas balance the body.

Each of us inherits a mix of all three doshas. Some dominate more than others, which is determined by many factors like your diet, family, and relationships. Understanding your dominant dosha helps you determine the right yoga routine and habits to practice in order to balance them.

"I get up, I fall down; meanwhile, I keep dancing."
– anonymous

reverse warrior

vata: (ether and air) Vata controls movement, breathing, and subtle energies. People for whom Vata is dominant tend to be in a hurry and have high energy. They are quick but forgetful. Vata people are chatty, indecisive, restless, active, and blow into a room like a tornado. They can be impulsive spenders and are highly creative. They get cold easily, and prefer cozy things like roaring fires and warm comforters. They have inconsistent eating and sleeping habits. Physically, Vata people are usually either very tall or very short with a thin build.

If your Vata is off, you might feel anxious, nervous, and particularly indecisive. You might develop dry skin or a lot of gas.

Yoga for Vatas: Slowing down and learning how to breathe is critical for you. Routines will help you feel grounded, so plan a morning and evening routine that you can stick by!

pitta: (fire and water) Pitta controls digestion, intelligence, and understanding. A Pitta person is competitive, self-motivated, precise, and goal-oriented. Their biggest challenge is not blowing a fuse—they tend to have angry outbursts. Pitta people are excellent public speakers, quick learners, and outspoken leaders. They are efficient with time and money, but will splurge on the occasional luxury. Physically, Pitta people have strong, athletic bodies, ruddy complexions, and a medium build. Almond-shaped eyes are another classic Pitta trait.

If Pitta is out of whack, you might develop skin rashes, get angry, obsess over things, or feel jealous.

Yoga for Pittas: Stop watching the person next to you! Start your practice in Savasana so you can develop inner awareness. Try to enjoy standing poses like Tree. Open up in Triangle Pose and feel blissful. Backbends and Camel will also help balance Pitta.

kapha: (earth and water) Kapha controls the body's secretions and resides in the chest. Kapha types are strong, methodical, healthy, and have a slow metabolism. They forgive and love easily. Kapha people speak and move slowly and are calm in nature. They save money. They love to eat. They have excellent memories and great endurance. They sleep well and dislike damp weather. Physically, Kaphas tend to have large frames, dark, thick, wavy hair, soft skin, and dark eyes.

If Kapha is out of whack, you might feel mentally sluggish and mildly depressed. You may put on weight easily and feel withdrawn or greedy.

Yoga for Kaphas: For Kaphas, developing a yoga practice helps circulation, metabolism, and self-esteem. Every day they need to exercise with walks, yoga, or anything to keep them stimulated. Sun Salutations and Warrior Poses are great for energizing a Kapha body.

dos and don'ts

Now that you know your yoga style, you might want to try a class setting to develop your practice. Although any yoga you've done at home will help prepare you for the poses that come up in class, the dynamic of a class is obviously different from stretching on your bedroom floor in pajamas. Don't worry—any class worth attending will be a nonjudgmental and welcoming place. But like anything, there are some unspoken rules of the road that will help you—and everyone around you—get the most out of class.

Do approach yoga with energy!

teach me

A great yoga teacher teaches from the heart and helps you discover your goodness. He or she should be knowledgeable about modified versions of each pose, and open to discussing your questions. She won't force a beginner into an advanced pose, but should encourage you to learn at your own pace. You should feel safe and inspired, and leave class feeling energized. If you don't feel comfortable, try another class. There are tons of teachers out there—one of them will be right for you.

DOs

Do arrive early. Getting to class a few minutes early allows you to mentally prepare. You can also get settled on your mat and stretch out in Child's Pose or limber up in Downward Dog.

Do practice on an empty stomach. An empty stomach allows you more freedom of movement in the poses. It also prevents embarrassing gas attacks!

Do come with a positive attitude and open mind. Every yoga class is different, so try not to judge too quickly and keep your mind open to the journey.

Do bring a bottle of water. It's important to stay hydrated during any kind of exercise. Keep a bottle by your mat so you can take a sip whenever you need it.

Do let your yoga teacher know of any injuries. Yoga teachers are trained to modify poses depending on their students' needs. If you have an injury, speak up!

Do ask for help when you need it. Speak up if you aren't sure about a pose. Yogis are a compassionate group—no one expects perfection.

Do try to be still in Savasana. Savasana can be the most difficult part of class, but it's even harder when someone fidgets beside you. Respect others' need for stillness at this part of the practice.

DON'Ts

Don't enter class late. Coming late or leaving early is disruptive, so try to avoid this if possible.

Don't bring a cell phone to your mat. If you have one, keep it at home or turned off in your bag. Cell phone rings in the middle of class are beyond annoying.

Don't try to dominate the class. Be respectful of your peers and don't try to grab the teacher's attention in every pose—others deserve her attention as well. Just enjoy where you are.

Don't push yourself too hard. Try to learn at your own pace and avoid comparison with others. It never matters how your form compares with your neighbor's—just practice with full-breath awareness to your individual edge.

Don't knock others. Avoid laughing at others when they are trying a new pose. It's everyone's job in yoga class to create an encouraging environment.

yoga journal

Nearly 2,000 years ago, an Indian yogi and physician named Pantanjali was the first to actually write about his yoga practice. His ancient text, The Yoga Sutras, played a huge role in introducing yoga to the world. That's why I always encourage my students to keep a journal; you never know when your thoughts and experiences can help others.

A journal can help you explore your emotions and let go of stress. Write about your embarrassing stories, jot down inspiring sayings, or just recount the events of your day. Think about how you feel before and after you practice. Does yoga change your mood? What thoughts bounce around when you're practicing? Do you feel powerful?

Why are you drawn to yoga? If you are not sure, try writing down how you feel after a yoga class and figure it out.

....
....
....

Think about the concept of ahisima, or non-violence. What does this mean to you? How can you be non-violent in your yoga practice and in your life?

....
....
....

Describe your boyfriend, girlfriend, or crush. Now reread your description. Do you still like this person?

....
....
....

Listing several adjectives, how would you describe yourself? How would your friends describe you? How would your family describe you? If you don't know, ask them.

....
....
....
....

Have you ever had a relationship that was stressful? How did your body and mind react to stress? List your symptoms.

What are some of your favorite yoga poses? List your favorites and try to describe how you feel after you try them.

What do you love about yourself? List everything!

Have you ever felt bored with your life? How would you reinvent yourself?

Do you know when others are jealous of you? How do they act? What makes you jealous? What do you think would help eliminate jealous feelings?

Try recording your dreams. What did you dream about this week that you remember? What do you think your dreams were trying to tell you?

karma check

Radiant angels are watching. I think we have spiritual guides or angels that help steer us in the right direction. Do you follow their advice? Better yet, are you yourself a guardian angel to others?

Karma is yoga in action. Karma is a Sanskrit word for the path of good deeds. Will your actions be kind and truthful or thoughtless and selfish? The path you choose creates your destiny. Karma builds up over time or washes away with bad behavior. Your deeds determine whether it ebbs or flows, so make every action count.

The practice of yoga opens your mind in a way that helps you feel compassion for others. It

"If you light a lamp for somebody, it will also brighten your path."

— *Buddhist saying*

butterfly

smile often

I have always tried to be myself, make friends, and get to know people of all ages. One day, my friend suggested I stop being so friendly or I'd get followed. I thought that she was crazy, so I continued waving and saying hello to every friendly face. Guess what? I have never been followed. Kindness spreads. Plus, all that smiling has gotten me extra cookies tossed in my bag, free parking, tick spray for my dog, tickets to the Red Sox, and other nice surprises. Of course, that's not why you do it, but I think people are just really grateful when you enjoy their company and make it pleasant for them.

"Kindness begets kindness."

– Greek Proverb

"Kindness is more than deeds. It is an attitude, an expression, a look, a touch."

– C. Neil Strait, writer (1934-2003)

helps you forge a path of self-realization and start to see new possibilities. It helps you put others first. Maybe your creativity can help others. Find a way to put your talents to work helping others in your community—volunteering at a daycare center, mentoring kids, visiting a nursing home. Put that compassion to work!

Kindness always rewards kindness. All those positive thoughts and actions will bounce back to help you. They can actually protect you from the negative thoughts that can haunt and hound you. Energy gets stuck when you say or even think negative or hateful thoughts, which can lead to emotional stress and even physical injury. Let yoga and karma release that stuck energy.

Don't just extend kindness to people, but to all living things. There are plenty of ways to help. In turn, your generosity helps you. It heals you. Trust me.

Om Gam Ganapataye Namaha

This mantra is pronounced *om gum gonna-pot-I-eh nah-ma-ha* and helps remove challenges in order to succeed in one's efforts. It helps you be successful.

yoga chicks

What makes people interesting? Passion. If you love to play the violin, make music passionately. If sports are your thing, play passionately. When you travel, explore passionately. There are soul mates all around the world waiting to meet you...even if for just a few minutes. And when they ask, share your life. Hey, introduce them to yoga—maybe they'll shine too!

laetitia   tyler   taylor   katherine

THE DRAMA QUEEN

People say I am: funny, smart, friendly.

Future Career: acting

Greatest Fear: something bad happening to my mom

Worst Habit: I bite my nails.

Love: math

Why Yoga: When I first tried yoga, it made me feel GREAT! It also helps me improve my balance and flexibility.

SPORTY GIRL

People say I am: kind, fun, a super soccer player.

Future Career: fashion designer

Love: to shop

Worst Habit: twirling my hair

People Don't Know: I'm bilingual.

Why Yoga: Yoga helps me stretch out, so I don't feel so tight from sports.

THE GOOD FRIEND

People say I am: lively thoughtful, centered

Greatest Fear: fear itself

Love: playing ice hockey, watching figure skating

Pet Peeve: when people don't wave when you stop your car for them

Greatest Talent: cheering people up

Why Yoga: I love sinking into poses that really help your mind. I do yoga for depression.

THE BRAIN

People say I am: quirky, curious, imaginative

Future Career: artist/bakery/gallery-owner in France

Favorite Color: black

Hobbies: pottery, yoga

People Don't Know: I have a pet hedgehog.

Worst Habit: not saying hello

Why Yoga: magnetic attraction

Can you match the yogi to their personality? If you guess wrong, not to worry—it's impossible to guess what someone is like from the way they look. It just goes to prove that you can never judge a book by its cover! That's one of life's great surprises about people.

jackie

christy

anna

mariana

FLIRTY GIRL

People say I am: fun, athletic, passionate

Future Career: business woman

Love: skiing with friends and family

Proud Fact: I am passionate about everything I do.

People Don't Know: I need two back-up alarms to get up.

Why Yoga: Yoga makes me feel light as if I have no worries or obligations.

FAMILY FIRST

People say I am: positive, caring, generous

Love: dancing

Interesting Fact: I love cooking while watching cooking shows.

Worst Habit: sleeping too much

Favorite Sport: volleyball

Why Yoga: I started doing yoga after my sister tried it and loved it.

THE ARTIST

People say I am: shy, humble, a gifted artist

Future Career: designer/artist

Love: giant vegetarian subs, playing guitar, dogs, tennis

Proud Fact: I have never told a lie.

People Don't Know: I'm a wild dancer.

Why Yoga: I started yoga when I was five. I love to let go of my thoughts and stretch.

THE OVERACHIEVER

People say I am: loyal, intelligent, athletic

Future Career: model

Greatest Fear: rejection

Favorite Food: Chinese

Greatest Talent: making friends

Why yoga: I was stressed. I like that anyone can do it, and it makes me calm.

yoga speak

Throughout this book, we've referred to poses by their English names. Many yoga classes use the Sanskrit names for poses, as well. Just in case your ancient languages need a little brushing up, here's a key to some terms you might hear in class:

Sanskrit Pose Names

Alana • Crescent Lunge

Apanasana • Knees to chest

Ardha Bhujangasana • Sphinx

Ardha Chandrasana • Half Moon

Ardha Matsyendrasana • Seated Spinal Twist

Ardha Navasana • Boat

Adho Mukha Svanasana • Downward Dog

Anjaneyasana • Runner's Lunge

Baddha Konasana • Butterfly

Bakasana • Crow

Balasana • Child's Pose

Bharadrajasana • Hero Twist

Bhekasana • Frog

Bhujangasana • Cobra

Chakravakasana • Cat

Chaturanga • Yoga Push Up

Chaturanga Dandasana • Plank

Chatushpada Pitham • Table

Dandasana • Mountain

Dhanurasana • Bow

Dwi pada rajakopotasana • Double Pigeon

Eka Pada Bakasana 2 • Crow/Firefly

Garudasana • Eagle

Gomukhasana • Cow Face

Halasana • Plow

Hasangasana • Rabbit Pose

Janu Sirsasana • Forward Bend

Jathara Parivartanasana • Reclining Knee Twist

Kapotasana variation • Pigeon

Matsyasana • Fish

Natarajasana • Dancer's Pose

Navasana • Boat

Padmasana • Lotus

Parsva Bakasana • Side Crow

Parsvottanasana • Pyramid

Parivrtta Parsvakonasan • Twisted Crescent Lunge

Paschimottanasana • Seated Forward Bend

Pincha Mayrasana • Dolphin

Prasarita Padottanasana • Straddle Split

Prstha Vakrasana • Leaning Mountain

Rajakapotasana • King Pigeon

Salamba Sirsasana • Headstand

Salamba Sarvangasana • Shoulder Stand

Savasana • Corpse

Setu Bandha Sarvangasana • Bridge

Sirsasana • Headstand

Sukhasana • Easy Pose

Tittibhasana • Firefly

Upavistha Konasana • Butterfly

Urdhva Dhanurasana • Wheel

Ustrasana • Camel

Utkatasana • Lightning Bolt

Uttanasana • Standing Forward Bend

Utthita Parsvakonasana • Extended Side Angle

Utthita Trikonasana • Triangle

Vimanasana • Airplane

Virabhadrasana 1 • Warrior One

Virabhadrasana 2 • Warrior Two

Virabhadrasana 2 variation • Reverse Warrior

Virabhadrasana 3 • Warrior Three

Vrksasana • Tree

Glossary

Asana	seat, physical pose
Ayurveda	the science of life, which is a practice in India that combines natural remedies with a personal approach to managing disease and dosha imbalance
Aura	electromagnetic energy fields that surround human beings
Bodhisattva	a Buddhist term for someone who is enlightened because they follow a path of helping others without expectation of a reward
Buddha	awakened, person who has attained enlightenment
Chakra	psycho-energetic center known as a wheel of the subtle body; five centers known in Buddhist yoga
Dosha	dominant traits that make up our physical and mental characteristics in ayurvedic yoga – the science of natural ways to good health
Drishti	a focal point or gaze of the eyes to one point
Karma	the yoga of action; the law of cause and effect
Lotus	symbol for enlightenment and mental purity; the Lotus roots in mud but blossoms one petal at a time into a beautiful flower
Mandala	a circular design used for meditation
Mantra	sacred sound or phrase that has a meditative effect on the mind
Mudra	hand gestures
Namaste	the universal prayer position meaning "the light in me, greets the light in you" said as a welcome or farewell in class
Om	a mantra symbolizing the sound of the world at peace
Pantanjali	Indian yogi and physician who is believed to be the founder of yoga
Prana	breath or life force
Samadhi	final goal of meditation
Sanskrit	an ancient Indian language
Sit bones	the boney part of your bottom that you can feel when you sit on a firm flat surface
Swami	respectful title for an enlightened teacher who attains master status
Ujjayi	victorious breath
Yoga	from yuj which means to yoke or join
Yogi	a person who practices yoga
Yogini	a female yogi

index

Resources

books:

Bancroft, Anne. 2000. *The Buddha Speaks*. Boston, MA: Shambhala Publications.

Boon, Brooke and Kirk, Martin. 2006. *Hatha Yoga Illustrated*. Champaign, IL: Human Kinetics.

Brown, Christina. 2003. *The Yoga Bible*. Cincinnati, OH: Godsfield Press.

Chryssicas, Mary Kaye. 2005. *I Love Yoga*. NY, NY: DK Publishing.

Cooper, Evan. 2005. *Um, Like...OM: A Girl Goddess's Guide to Yoga*. NY, NY: Little, Brown Young Readers.

Deger, Steve and Gibson, Leslie Ann. 2006. *The Little Book of Positive Quotations*. Minneapolis: Fairview Press.

Desikachar, T.K.V. 1995. *The Heart of Yoga*. Rochester, NY: Inner Traditions International.

Faulds, Richard. 2006. *Kripalu Yoga: A Guide to Practice On and Off the Mat*. NY, NY: Bantam Dell.

Finger, Alan. 2005. *Chakra Yoga: Balancing Energy for Physical, Spiritual and Mental Well-Being*. Boston, MA: Shambhala Publications.

Fontana, David. 1999. *Learn to Meditate*. San Francisco, CA: Chronicle Books.

Gallanis, Bess. 2006. *Yoga Chick: A Hip Guide to Everything Om*. NY, NY: Warner Books.

Gannon, Sharon and Life, David. 2002. *Jivamukti Yoga*. NY, NY: The Ballantine Publishing Group.

Iyengar, B.K.S. 2001. *Yoga: The Path to Holistic Health*. London: DK Publishing.

Kabat-Zinn, Jon. 1994. *Wherever You Go There You Are*. NY, NY: Hyperion.

Khalsa, Shakta Kaur. 2002. *Yoga for Women*. NY, NY: DK Publishing.

Lark, Liz. 2001. *Yoga for Life*. London: Carlton Books.

Lark, Liz. 2003. *Yoga for Kids*. Buffalo New York: Firefly Books.

Luby, Thia. 1999. *Yoga for Teens*. Santa Fe, New Mexico: Clear Light Publishers.

Phillips, Kathy. 2001. *The Spirit of Yoga*. Hauppauge, NY: Barron's Educational Services.

Rappaport, Julie. 2004. *365 Yoga Daily Meditations*. NY, NY: Penguin Books.

Satchidananda, Sri Swami. 1990. *The Yoga Sutras of Patanjali*. Buckingham, VA: Integral Yoga Publications.

Silas, Elizabeth and Goodney, Diane. 2003. *Yoga*. NY, NY: Scholastic.

Schwartz, Ellen. 2003. *I Love Yoga: A Guide for Kids and Teens*. Toronto, Ontario: Tundra Books.

Sparrowe, Linda. 2002. *Yoga: A Yoga Journal Book*. Berkeley, CA: Hugh Lauter Levin Associates, Inc.

Yee, Rodney and Nina Zolotow. 2004. *Moving Toward Balance*. NY, NY: Rodale.

guides:

Brock, Christy and Lightsey, Jennifer.
Yoga 4 Teens: An Instructor's Guide for Teaching Yoga to Teenagers.

magazines:

Body and Soul • Fit Yoga • Natural Health
Yoga Magazine • Yoga Journal • Yoga + Joyful Living
Yoga Journal was a valuable resource in researching this book.

websites:

www.yoga4teens.com • www.yogajournal.com
www.buddhafulkids.com • www.kripalu.org
www.yogamagazine.co.uk • www.ayurveda.com
www.karmaresources.com • www.amsa.org
www.dalailamafoundation.org • www.yogalliance.org

quotes:

Deger, Steve and Gibson, Leslie Ann. 2006. *The Little Book of Positive Quotations*. Minneapolis: Fairview Press. Gandhi: p. 115
Lauren Dillon t-shirt, Hamm, p. 120
Degeneres, Ellen. 2006. The Ellen Degeneres Show, p. 120
Digha Nikaya, p. 110
Mandukya Upanishad, p. 25
www.heartquotes.net, W.H. Auden: p. 113
www.quotations.about.com, Strait: p. 155
www.soulfuture.com, Holtz: p. 74, Epicetus: p. 22
www. Motivational-inspirational-corner.com, Lao Tzu: p. 44
www.Thinkexist.com, Shaw: p. 86
www.quotationspage.com, Kipling, p. 94, Colette: p. 109
www.quotegarden.com, Dr. Seuss, p. 96
www.brainyquote.com, Dryden: p.99, Krishnamurti: p.116
www.coolquotes.com, Peale: p.14

acknowledgments

DK Publishing would like to thank the following for their help with this book:
Tyler Chryssicas, Laetitia Mead, Anna Cosimini, Christy Adler, Katherine Kyrios, Taylor Mobley, Jackie Tayabji, Mariana Ley and back-up models Liz McNeill and Elizabeth Gray. And a very special thanks to Tyler and Laetitia for performing on the DVD.

From the author: Heartfelt gratitude to my editor, Beth Hester, for breathing life into this book and world with the arrival of Sophie! Thanks also to soul sisters Michelle Baxter, Angela Coppola, Jessica Park, and all the great minds behind the scenes at DK.

Thanks to my husband, Ted, who is in a constant state of bodhisattva by demonstrating daily acts of kindness without ever expecting anything in return. To my dad, Patrick Milmoe, whose great sense of humor entertains all, my mom, Kay Milmoe, for putting up with my wild antics over the years, and my siblings, Caroline and Hugh. Giant hugs to Tyler, Ashton and Grant – who entered the world radiating sunshine. Your genuine kindness to all you meet, enthusiasm, and unique spirits inspire me. Thanks for your patience while I explore my creativity and burn your dinners. To Brooke, Susie, Oriet, Brett, Hillary, Suzanne, Donna, Carolyn, Leslie, Cups, Sue, Mary R., Laurel, Heather, Whitney, and Sherri for belly ache laughs. To Susu Aylward for feeding the yogis and spreading sunshine. To Mary Sullivan, Christine Goss, and Heather Knopf for their encouragement! And to Vanderbilt friends and Collegiate pals from the teen years in Richmond, Virginia! Thank you teen yogis – I love your positive energy and cherish your friendships. And to parents, thank you for sending all those buddhaful yogis my way – especially Murphy who dares to be different. I love y'all!

About the Author

Just as she does in her popular yoga classes, Mary Kaye Chryssicas speaks to teens with an easy mix of respect, compassion, and humor. With real sensitivity to teen issues such as eating disorders, low self-esteem, body image, and peer pressure, Mary Kaye uses yoga to help teens find confidence and respect for their own minds and bodies. Mary Kaye has studied many different styles of yoga including Hatha, Ashtanga, Kundalini, Anusara, and Iyengar. She is an internationally recognized teacher of yoga for children of all ages and a registered yoga teacher with Yoga Alliance. She has taught and coached children in sports and yoga programs for over 15 years. Mary Kaye brings her insightful, funny, and enthusiastic spirit plus extensive yoga study to her teachings. She is also the author of, *I Love Yoga*, a DK children's book. Before discovering yoga, Mary Kaye was an advertising director for several magazines. She lives passionately, laughs often, and dances wildly in Boston with three bendy kids, a husband who can't touch his toes, and an untrained vizsla. Mary Kaye can be reached at mkchryssicas@comcast.net or www.buddhafulkids.com.

Namaste.

To get a free packet of heirloom vegetable seeds from the author, go to the "Free Offers" tab at SeedRenaissance.com.

120   NOTES

The Secret to Pizza-Making

I've made a lot of homemade pizza over the years—hundreds of pizzas at least. There is one trick to making the best-flavored pizza: fresh, raw, minced onion. I always put about a tablespoon of minced onion on the top of the pizza as the last ingredient. Perennial Egyptian Walking Onions are perfect for this (for information on these onions, see my first book, The Forgotten Skills of Self-Sufficiency Used by the Mormon Pioneers. *I also sell bulb sets for these perennial onions at my website, SeedRenaissance.com). There is something about the baked, minced onion that just brings out all the other flavors, no matter what kind of pizza you are making. So good!*

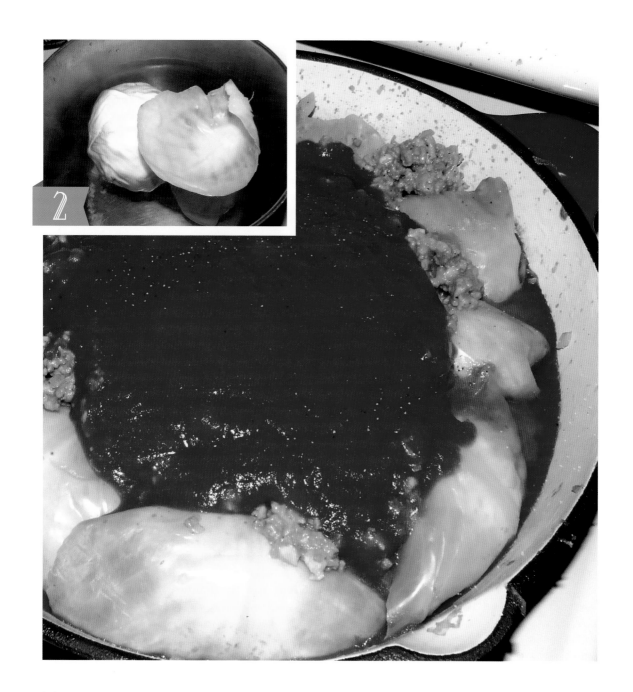

Stuffed
Cabbage Limousin

SERVES 4-6

Limousin is a region in southwest France that has been called the country's rural heartland. The area is famed for its Limousin beef, which my family raised for beef on our farm in Utah when I was a child (among other breeds). Limousin cuisine is said to be famed for its traditional rustic flavor and its use of the region's beef. Today, few people seem to make stuffed cabbage anymore, but it is certainly a dish that is worth cooking.

1 lb. ground beef or ground pork, or half and half

1 onion

1 cabbage

2 cups Roman Tomato Sauce (see recipe in this book)

1 clove garlic (optional)

½ cup breadcrumbs

1 egg

1 to 2 cups of cooked rice (optional)

salt

pepper

1   Brown meat and onions together.

2   Meanwhile, bring a stockpot of water to a boil. Place a clean head of cabbage into the water for 40 seconds. Remove from water and peel the outer leaf from the head. Repeat until you have a dozen large leaves. Trim the main stem of each leaf by cutting the stem in half along the leaf.

3   Warm tomato sauce in skillet.

4   In a bowl, mix meat, breadcrumbs, egg, and seasoning. Adding cooked rice will allow you to stuff larger portions. Place a quarter-cup to a half-cup of mix inside each cabbage leaf. Fold leaf closed around stuffing and place in the skillet of tomato sauce. Simmer on low with cover for 30 minutes. Enjoy!

Roman Tomato Sauce

My son-in-law, Trent Lott, lived in the Rome region of Italy for two years, and he taught me to make delicious sauce. This sauce is savory beyond belief because it cooks for two hours! If you don't want to make the traditional 2-hour version, cut the cooking time to 20 minutes.

2½ cups tomato purée

½ teaspoon dried basil

¼ teaspoon dried oregano

¼ teaspoon dried marjoram

¼ teaspoon dried thyme

¼ teaspoon dried parsley

¼ teaspoon dried cilantro

¼ teaspoon dried savory (summer or winter variety)

Two carrots, finely shredded

½ teaspoon salt

1 stalk of celery

2 tablespoons olive oil

1½ teaspoons salt

1 In a saucepan, mix all ingredients and bring to a boil.

2 Once the mixture is at a boil, lower the heat to the lowest setting possible, cover the pan, and cook for two hours, stirring about every 20 minutes.

Crockpot Squash Casserole

7-8 cups chopped summer squash

1 chopped onion

3 shredded carrots

1 cup chicken stock

2 cups sour cream

1 package panko breadcrumbs

4 oz. grated parmesan cheese

1   Mix squash, onion, carrots, stock, and sour cream in crockpot. Cook on low for 3 hours.

2   After three hours, stir in ¾ of the bag of breadcrumbs and 3 oz. of cheese. Spread remaining cheese and breadcrumbs on top of the casserole. Cook one more hour on low in crockpot, or transfer removeable crockpot casserole dish to oven for 15 minutes on 375 degrees.

Winter Stew

SERVES 4–6
PREPARATION AND COOK TIME: 30 MINUTES

Hands down, nothing is better on a cold winter's day than a dish of this stew. Well, okay, there is one thing better--a serving of popovers on the side (see the recipe in this book), to eat with the gravy in true English fashion!

1½ lb. of stew meat, cut into half-inch cubes

½ cup olive oil

½ cup whole-wheat flour

3 onions, chopped

4 cups hot water

3 medium potatoes

4 carrots

1 teaspoon salt

2 tablespoons all-natural beef bouillon

1. Begin heating the oil over medium-high heat in a large soup pot. Meanwhile, in a bowl, toss the beef cubes and the flour until the beef is coated. Pour the beef cubes and any remaining flour into the hot oil and stir until the beef is seared.

2. Immediately reduce the heat to medium and add in the chopped onions. Stir and cook until the onions are just beginning to be tender.

3. Add water and remaining ingredients. Stir while bringing to a boil. Reduce heat to a strong simmer and stir occasionally. Cook until vegetables are tender. Taste before serving and adjust the salt or bouillon as needed. Serve hot.

Creamy Carrot Butternut Soup—In a Crockpot!

For this recipe, take any winter squash and put it in your crockpot on low overnight with ¾-inch of water. If you put in a whole squash, like a potimarron, twist a steak knife into the squash to make a single hole to vent the steam. If you have a larger squash, you can cut it into large chunks just to fit it into the crockpot. When the squash is cooked, dispose of skin and seeds. If you don't want to use the overnight method, you can cut up a squash and boil it until tender, about 30 minutes.

1 medium butternut or other
　winter squash, cooked

1 cup cream

2 cups chicken broth

½ teaspoon salt

7 carrots, finely diced

1 onion, chopped

1　Put broth, salt, chopped onion, cream, and cooked pumpkin into blender for 10 seconds.

2　Put pumpkin mixture into a crockpot on low. Add carrots. Cook 3-4 hours.

Slow Cooker Carrot Zucchini Lasagna

If you are not familiar with slicing-by-peeler, you are missing out! This is one of my favorite ways to serve vegetables, because it is unusual and unexpected, fun to do, and so easy! All you do is take a carrot or zucchini, and use your peeler to turn your vegetable into long, thin strips , like lasagna noodles. This technique is especially great for adding carrots to salads. In this crockpot recipe, our long, thin strips of carrots and zucchini become our lasagna noodles. Note that this recipe uses oven-ready lasagna noodles, which are not boiled before using.

3 medium zucchini, sliced with a peeler

4 carrots, sliced with a peeler

1 medium onion, finely chopped (or 2–3 shallots)

1½ cups whole tomatoes, blended to juice

1 teaspoon salt

½ teaspoon ground black pepper

1 teaspoon dried leaf basil OR small handful of fresh basil leaves

½ cup grated Parmesan cheese

1 cup grated Swiss cheese

1 lb. beef or sweet Italian sausage, browned (or half and half)

1 package oven-ready lasagna noodles

1 Peel carrots and zucchini and add the strips to your crockpot with the chopped onions.

2 Put tomatoes in blender and turn to sauce. Add basil, salt, and pepper, and pulse for a few seconds. Pour mixture over noodles in crockpot.

3 Cook 3 hours on low in crockpot.

4 Top with Swiss cheese and cook for another 1½ to 2 hours in crockpot on low.

Carrot & Hubbard Squash Soup

SERVES 4–6
PREPARATION AND COOK TIME:
30 MINUTES

One squash the size of a bowling ball makes four quarts of this soup. This is wonderful for a rainy or snowy day and doesn't take much time to make. This recipe is totally self-provident and adaptable. You could add tabasco sauce to make it spicy if you wanted, or cream after taking the soup of the stove if you want a sweeter soup.

1 Put cooked squash into blender, one quarter of the squash at a time, with ½ cup of the broth each time. Purée.

2 In the final batch of squash purée, add in the onion and purée the onion with the squash.

3 In a large soup pot, add the purée and all other ingredients. Cook until vegetables are tender, about 30 minutes. Enjoy!

1 hubbard or other winter squash, cooked

2 cups vegetable broth

1 onion, quartered

1 teaspoon salt

4 carrots, finely diced

2 leeks, trimmed and finely diced

2 potatoes, finely diced

Tomato Basil Corn Chowder

SERVES 4–6
PREPARATION AND COOK TIME:
30 MINUTES

Tomatoes (whole, fresh, enough to fill a blender)

30-40 fresh basil leaves (or 2 table-spoons dried)

5 carrots

2 large beets (I use Albino Sugar or Chioggia varieties)

corn (cut from 4-6 ears)

1 onion

2 leeks (optional)

8 oz. (half a box) spiral macaroni (or your favorite kind)

2 cups summer squash

1 Fill a blender with fresh whole tomatoes and a small handful of basil leaves and a cup of water. Purée. Put this mixture into a pot and bring to a boil.

2 Dice (or julienne) carrots, beets, onions, and leeks, and add to the soup. Add 5 cups of water and bring to a boil again.

3 Put in macaroni. Cook until macaroni is tender. Vegetables should also be tender.

4 Add chopped squash. Cook for 90 seconds. Turn off heat. Enjoy!

Winter Pumpkin Bake

Pumpkins are not all the same. Halloween pumpkins, which are usually the Connecticut Field variety, are thin-walled and not generally sweet-fleshed. For the best baking pumpkin, I suggest Potimarron or Mormon Pumpkin. Potimarron is teardrop-shaped with deep red skin and thick orange flesh that is sweet. Mormon Pumpkin is a variety from antiquity saved from extinction by SeedRenaissance.com. The mature pumpkin is dusky green on the outside with bright, sweet and thick orange flesh inside. You can also use butternut or banana squash in this recipe, or any favorite baking squash.

1 baking pumpkin or winter squash

Butter

Garam masala Indian spice blend

1   Heat the oven to 375 degrees. Wash the pumpkin. Near the top of the pumpkin, twist the tip of a sharp knife into the flesh until you have created a hole that pierces through to the center of the pumpkin.

2   Fill a glass or stoneware casserole dish with a half-inch of water. Put the whole pumpkin into the dish so that it sits in the water. Put the dish into the oven for 60–80 minutes, or until you see a brown spot develop on the side of the pumpkin that begins to collapse. Remove from

the oven, being careful not to splash or spill the water in the baking dish.

3   Using hot pads, remove the pumpkin from the baking dish and put it on large serving dish. Cut the pumpkin in half. Using a large spoon, scrape the seeds and fiber from the center of the pumpkin.

4   Cut a shallow criss-cross pattern in the flesh with a knife. Rub the flesh with butter. Sprinkle lightly with garam masala spice blend. Serve hot.

Thorrablot Mash

SERVES 4–6

I am going to admit two things right up front. First, this is one of my favorite foods of all time. Second, I got this recipe, after some begging, from the chef who was catering one of the famous Thorrablot Icelandic Viking Midwinter Feasts in Spanish Fork, Utah, hosted each winter by the Icelandic Association of Utah. (A bunch of Icelanders settled in Utah.) If you've never had a chance to go to a Thorrablot (you can find them across the U.S.), then you should. In Utah, they bring in truly old traditional foods for people to try: cured shark, haddock and lamb. And rutabagas.

Rutabagas are out of favor in the U.S. for some reason that is inexplicable to me. They are growing in my autumn garden as I write this, and have been since my first Thorrablot feast more than a decade ago. Rutabagas, called swedes in Great Britain, are the prime ingredient in Cornish Pasty, as you have already seen in this cookbook. These light-orange, round roots have a flavor that is half-carrot and half-parsnip. Once you have tasted Thorrablot Mash, you will never go back to regular old mashed potatoes again. In fact, you will wonder why we haven't been eating the Icelandic way all these years!

This version of mashed potatoes is lightly sweet and also light-orange in color. From a glycemic standpoint, Thorrablot Mash is also far healthier for you than mashed potatoes. Even though I have provided a recipe below, this is really a "ratio recipe," meaning you can make this recipe in any size as long as you use roughly equal amounts of the three vegetables. In the rare chance that you have leftover Thorrablot Mash, you can use it in the Kyoto Croquettes recipe in this book.

3 rutabagas	salt
3 potatoes	pepper
6 carrots	butter

1 Steam or boil the vegetables.

2 Mash or blend the vegetables, making them smooth or chunky according to personal taste. Add butter, salt, and pepper to taste. Serve warm, with or without gravy.

Traditional Shabu-Shabu

This is possibly the most beloved dish in Japanese cuisine, and there are specialty restaurants around the U.S.–even where I live in Utah–that specialize in serving nothing else. The concept is elegant in its simplicity. A pot of boiling broth or stock is put in the center of the table, within reach of everyone. Family-style plates around the table are piled with fresh raw meats (paper-thin) and vegetables. A pot of warm rice is always served. Everyone picks their own meat and vegetable and cooks them in the pot of broth and then eats them on top of the rice. It's a great party meal, and a particularly great way to celebrate the New Year, either on Jan. 1 or on the Chinese New Year. We have celebrated both with shabu-shabu.

You can get an electric shabu-shabu pan from Amazon.com starting at about $25, and if you love to eat fresh, it is worth the investment. If you don't have a pan, you can use a crockpot.

A note about shabu-shabu meat. In order to cook in just a couple minutes, shabu-shabu meat is tra-

ditionally served in almost paper-thin slices. Pork loin, beef loin, and chicken breast are usually all served as part of shabu-shabu, with guests choosing their preference. Shabu-shabu meat can be found in the freezer section of most Asian food stores but it not typically found in grocery stores. I have, on several occasions, gone to our local grocery store butcher and asked them to partially freeze the meat I was buying from them and then slice it as thin as they could get it. (They had never heard of shabu-shabu meat, and I had to explain the concept to them, but they sliced it as I asked.)

As a serving size, provide 4–6 ounces of meat per person and 6-10 ounces of vegetables per person. Duck, crab, and lobster may also be used. I have listed the traditional ingredients below, but you can be creative and use whatever your family or guests will love.

2 quarts beef or chicken stock (or more, depending on the size of your pot)

Pork loin (raw and thin-sliced)

Beef ribeye or sirloin (raw and thin-sliced)

Chicken breast (raw and thin-sliced)

Carrots (julienned)

Summer squash (sliced)

Asian cabbage (shredded)

Turnips (sliced)

Diakon radish (sliced)

Enoki mushrooms (or any favorite mushroom)

Tofu (cubed)

Buckwheat noodles

cooked rice (1 cup per person)

Gyoza sauce (for dipping; see the recipe in this book) OR

prepared shabu-shabu sauce OR soy sauce

Fifteen Mouth-Watering Twists on Egg Salad Sandwiches

Basic Egg Salad

At our house, my wife often keeps hard-boiled eggs in the fridge. The grandkids love to eat them plain and I love to make egg salad sandwiches, especially for lunch or a quick midnight snack. Sandwiches are best on homemade bread or multi-grain bread from the store. I prefer the bread untoasted but to each their own. This recipe is for basic egg salad, which most people are familiar with, but I include it here because it is the foundational recipe for all of the options that follow.

1 hard-boiled egg

1 tablespoon best quality plain mayonnaise

pinch of salt

pinch of pepper

1 Slice the egg into pieces and mash with a fork.

2 Stir in the mayonnaise and spices. Spread over bread or toast and enjoy.

1 Parmesan cheese.
A tablespoon of grated parmesan instantly changes the flavor of an egg salad sandwich, making it more savory and sophisticated.

2 Melted Parmesan Disc.
Put two tablespoons parmesan in the center of a nonstick frying pack on low heat. Melt until the cheese becomes crusty. Remove from the pan and place the disc of cheese over the egg salad on an open-faced sandwich.

3 Ground Summer Squash.
Take half of a small summer squash and mince it or grind it in a food processor. Add to the basic egg salad recipe.

4 Stuffed Popover Sandwich.
Instead of using bread, stuff your egg salad into a cooled Altitude Popover from the recipe in this cookbook.

5 Apple Gjetost. Gjetost is brown Norwegian cheese that looks and tastes like caramel.

For an egg salad sandwich that is as unusual as it is unforgettable, put a slice of gjetost on a slice of fresh apple, topped with a heaping tablespoon of egg salad. Don't use pepper in your egg salad for this recipe, as it doesn't go well with the apple and cheese.

6 Bacon Crumbles and Havarti Cheese. Havarti is a mild Danish cheese that is probably my favorite cheese in the world. It pairs especially well with bacon crumbles in egg salad. Havarti is fairly soft and does not grate easily, so you will want to mince a slice for one sandwich.

7 Dill. The light, bright flavor of dill weed goes well with egg salad, especially in summer. Add a pinch of fresh or dried dill to the basic egg salad recipe.

8 Coriander & Turmeric. Coriander is the seed of the cilantro plant, but it tastes nothing like cilantro. Add a ¼ teaspoon of crushed or ground coriander and an ⅛ teaspoon of turmeric to the basic recipe for a sandwich that is bright yellow with a savory flavor. Turmeric is also renowned as a natural anti-inflammatory, which is something anyone who eats sugar needs (sugar promotes chronic inflammation).

9 Diced Deli Cold Cuts. Add diced

ham or chicken to your sandwich, especially on a chilly winter afternoon.

10 Egg Salad Wraps. Use any of the above recipes as filler for a wrap. Add spinach if desired. Use warmed flour tortillas or pita for the wrap.

11 Naan. This traditional Indian flatbread is now widely found in grocery stores, in both white and whole wheat varieties. Sometimes naan is also available in flavors including sun-dried

tomato or garlic. Naan is best when warmed in a toaster oven. Tear the warm flatbread and use the egg salad as a dip.

12 Minced celery or Swiss Chard Ribs.
Add a tablespoon or two of these raw vegetables to any sandwich to make it crunchy.

13 Raw Minced Onion.
I will admit that this is not my favorite way to eat egg salad, but some people swear by it, so I include it here. A shallot onion is best. You can also add this to the celery or chard rib option above.

14 Curried Salad.
If you are in an exotic mood, add a pinch of curry powder to the basic recipe and serve on naan flatbread.

15 Lemon Zest & Chopped Thyme.
This works best with fresh thyme. A pinch of lemon zest and a pinch of thyme are enough for one sandwich. Sprinkle the zest carefully and mix it well to ensure there are no clumps in the salad.

5

Caleb's Ultra-Low Sugar Jam

MAKES APPROX. 2 PINTS OF JAM
COOK TIME: APPROX. 60 MINUTES

I have been using this jam recipe exclusively for more than 20 years. I love homemade jam, especially in winter, at breakfast on toast made of homemade bread. I had a real problem with traditional jam recipes because they called for more sugar than fruit. This has never tasted right to me, and it never felt healthy to eat. I wanted my jam to taste fresh from the garden. This recipe is the perfect answer. The flavor is sweet and fresh but not cloying.

9 cups of fresh berries or fresh chopped fruit juice of one lime

⅔ cup sugar

1 Preheat oven to 375 degrees. Mix ingredients into 9 x 13 glass casserole dish. Bake in oven at 375 degrees for 20 minutes. Reduce heat to 325 degrees. Stir fruit or berry mixture.

2 Cook for another hour, stirring every 20 minutes. Do a spoon test. If it fails, cook another 20 minutes. (Notice there is no pectin in this recipe!) Put jam in half-pint jars in the freezer.

How to do a spoon test

Plate Method: Put a stoneware, ceramic, or glass plate into the freezer before you begin cooking your jam. To test the jam, remove the cold plate from the freezer. Take a spoonful of jam from the oven and drop it gently on the frozen plate. Draw the tip of a spoon through the jam, creating a valley through the jam. If the valley stays, the jam is finished cooking. If the valley runs back together, the jam is not thick enough and needs to continue cooking.

Juice Can Method: Before you begin cooking jam, take a can of frozen juice concentrate from the freezer. With a clean towel, wash one of the metal ends of the can and put it back in the freezer. To test the jam, remove the frozen can from the freezer and set it on a hard surface with a metal side up. Take a spoonful of jam from the oven and drop it gently on the frozen metal side. Draw the tip of a spoon through the jam, creating a valley through the jam. If the valley stays, the jam is finished cooking. If the valley runs back together, then the jam is not thick enough and needs to continue cooking.

Ambrosia Jam

MAKES APPROX. 2 PINTS OF JAM
COOK TIME: APPROX. 60 MINUTES

This is one of my most requested recipes because I give tastings of this jam at some of my autumn classes. This recipe was born of necessity. The only cantaloupe I grow in my garden is called Noir des Carmes. It is a very old, rare, and enormously prolific melon. Noir des Carmes is one of the earliest melons to ripen and turns from dark green to orange literally overnight when it is ripe, so you never have to guess at when to pick it. Best of all, it never needs black plastic in my garden. My problem was that by the end of August, we had cantaloupe coming out of our ears to the point that we got sick of eating it. So I created this recipe, and now we have Ambrosia Jam all through the winter and spring. The flavor is bright, and the taste is garden fresh. We love it.

4½ cups ripe diced cantaloupe, rind removed

4½ cups ripe diced peaches, skins removed

⅔ cup sugar

juice of one lime

To cook, follow the instructions for the previous recipe in this book, Caleb's Ultra-Low Sugar Jam.

Charmayne's Easiest-Ever, Best-Ever Grape Juice

We make about 100 quarts of homemade grape juice a year, using our backyard grapes. We have probably tried every recipe out there, but this recipe is by far the easiest and fastest—and the only recipe I have been able to find that produces crystal-clear juice. Whenever our homemade grape juice is on our table, you know it is a special day. If we're celebrating, mourning, or gathering from afar, we serve homemade grape juice (usually four quarts at a sitting!) All large stems should be removed, but small pieces of stem (¼ inch or less) will not affect the flavor. You can drive yourself crazy trying to remove every last tiny bit of stem. The good news is that you don't need to bother. We use white grapes, Concord-type grapes, and rose grapes for making juice. Rose grapes are the most beautiful in the bottle.

Triple-washed backyard grapes (seeded or seedless), stems mostly removed

⅛ cup sugar per jar

1 Fill clean quart-sized canning jars half-full with whole, fresh grapes. Add sugar. Fill with hot tap water. Close jars with lids and rings.

2 Process in a boiling water bath for 10 minutes if your city is at 3,000 feet altitude or lower, or 15 minutes if you are at 3,000 feet or higher. (We live at 5,200 feet in the Rocky Mountains and we process for 15 minutes.) The jars should be covered with a half-inch of water in the bath. As altitude increases, water boils at a lower temperature (below 212 degrees). Lower temperatures are not as effective when it comes to destroying microorganisms that can cause food spoilage and illness. For this reason, you must add extra minutes at altitude.

3 Store the grape juice in a cool, dry place in your house away from sunlight. (A basement cold room is ideal) Let the grape juice sit for at least three months to mature. We wait until Thanksgiving at least. Strain out the grapes, add water to taste, and serve with ice. (Note: In winter, the kids gobble up the spent grapes that we strain out. They love to eat them, seeds and all.)

Note 1: Whether this is a recipe for concentrate is hotly debated at my house. I like to add a quart of water to a quart of our homemade grape juice, but some people like to drink it undiluted. The undiluted version is cloying to me.

Note 2: To make a super-concentrated grape juice, add ¼-cup of sugar per quart jar and then

fill the bottle to within one inch of the rim with grapes. Fill with hot tap water and follow the recipe as above. When serving, I add water enough to make three quarts of grape juice from this concentrate.

Note 3: To make sure your jars seal properly, always wipe the rim of the jar clean before putting on the lid. This removes any sugar granules that could prevent the jar from sealing. Jars that do not seal in the water bath can be reprocessed or stored in the fridge and used within 1–2 days.

Note 4: Naturally occurring tartaric acid sometimes forms crystals in the bottom of jars of homemade grape juice. Anyone who finds one in a jar at our house is considered lucky. The crystals take on the color of the juice, and can be up to an inch in size. If the crystal is large, the kids always want to keep it. Because this recipe makes clear juice, it rarely makes tartaric acid crystals, but they do still sometimes occur. They are harmless but not tasty to eat and should be removed from the juice.

How to Clean Grapes for Juicing

Put a tall pot filled with grapes, in the kitchen sink. Fill the pot with cold water and leave the water running in a small stream so the pot is constantly overflowing into the sink. This lets leaves and bits of stem float out as you sort the grapes. Any grapes that float to the surface should be discarded. In addition, do not use any grape that is squishy or has a hard texture on the skin. The best grapes are plump and supple. The size of the grape does not matter, so long as it is ripe. Grapes with seeds have a sweeter flavor than grapes without seeds.

Tips & Tricks

Preserving Tomatoes By Freezing (Two Methods)

Method 1 Wash fresh, ripe tomatoes. Remove stems. Pack whole tomatoes into a freezer bag. Close and seal. To use these tomatoes later, partially unthaw the tomatoes at room temperature. Put the semi-frozen tomatoes into the blender one at a time to make tomato sauce, or chop the tomatoes to use in stew, soup, Vegetable Masala Roll, or other recipes.

Method 2 We keep dozens of bags of raw tomato purée in our freezer throughout the year to use for making many of the dishes in this book, and more. We don't can tomatoes because freezing them is so much easier. Wash ripe tomatoes from the garden or local farm stand. Remove stems. One at a time, put the tomatoes in a blender and purée them. Sieve out the seeds if desired. (I don't remove the seeds because the seeds contain a lot of protein.) Pour 2½ cups raw purée into a quart-sized freezer bag. Seal the bag, leaving some air space inside. Tomato purée expands as it freezes and will need this air space. Lay the sealed bags flat on a cookie sheet and put them in the freezer. Remove the cookie sheet after the bags are frozen solid. Thaw at room temperature, in hot water, or in a microwave as needed.

How to Purée Tomatoes

The best tomato purée comes from meaty tomatoes with few seeds, such as Amish Paste, Roma, or German Queen (pictured).

1 To make purée, take fresh tomatoes from the garden and rinse them in cold water. If the tomato is a roma-type, cut the top off. If the tomato is a flat-type like German Queen, core the tomato.

2 Place a metal mesh strainer over a glass bowl. Cut the bottom fifth of the tomato off. Holding the tomato over the strainer, squeeze the tomato firmly so that the seeds come out into the strainer and the juice goes through the strainer into the bowl.

3 Open up the crushed tomato and rinse off remaining seeds in the sink and add it to the bowl. Continue until all your tomatoes have been deseeded.

4 Purée the tomatoes in the blender, starting on the lowest setting of the blender and moving up to the highest "liquefy" setting as the tomatoes begin to become more and more liquid. Use immediately or freeze in a glass canning jar or double-bag in freezer bags. If using a glass canning jar for freezing, fill only three quarters full to allow purée room to expand as it freezes.

Two Ways to Peel a Fresh Backyard Egg

The virtues of fresh backyard eggs are many, but as anyone with chickens knows, there is a downside to fresh eggs: when hard boiled, they are difficult to peel. I've had a lot of people ask me for advice. Here are two solutions:

Method 1 If you need to use your hard-boiled eggs immediately, this method is for you: After hard boiling your eggs, tap and roll the eggs on a hard surface like your kitchen counter until the shells are very cracked--but not so hard that you actually break up the hard-boiled egg inside. There will be a small air pocket at one end of the egg. After your shell is cracked, this air pocket should be evident. Carefully and slowly slide your thumb into the air pocket and down the side of the egg. The goal is to get your thumbnail under the shell. Then, use your thumbnail to peel circularly around the egg–never down, always around. If you try to peel down from the air pocket, you will have trouble. If your peel circularly, taking a bit at a time with your thumb, you will be able to peel the entire egg without having chunks of egg stuck to the shell. If chunks start to stick, you are going too fast. Slow down.

Method 2 This is my preferred method because it's much easier. Simply hard-boil your eggs and leave them in the fridge for two or three days, then follow the method above. You will be able to peel the whole egg much easier and faster.

Questions and Accusations (cough!) for the Author

Question: Confess! Your wife really does most of the cooking and you just take most of the credit!

Answer: That wasn't really so much of a question as it was an accusation. But I'll have to let that slide because this exact question (with almost this exact accusatory tone) has been posed to me at several book signings. The answer is, simply, that my wife is not a big cook. As I said earlier, she'd be pretty much thrilled to have a hard-boiled egg for lunch everyday for the rest of her life. I would not be happy with that menu. There is a now-infamous story in our family about the day my wife hollered at me because I wanted to eat a third meal. To this day, if my wife says anything about not wanting to eat (which isn't unusual for her) the kids break in with a chorus of "You want three meals a day?!" quoting that infamous moment. We all laugh about it, but it is true that my wife is a tiny leaf that could be blown away in a stiff wind, and I'm six-foot-four and I LOVE to eat.

So I cook most of the time.

My wife does bottle peaches and grape juice with me (she taught me how to bottle grape juice—that is one thing I don't recall my ever seeing my parents, grandparents, or great-grandparents do). But I make the jams and jellies, I make the bread, and I make 80 percent of our lunches and dinners. And we don't agree on everything. She has either cold cereal or hot oatmeal for breakfast. I don't believe in cold cereal any more (the prices got too high, the boxes got too light and the sugar too sugary), and I especially don't believe anyone should be feeding cold cereal to children, especially before sending them to school, because cold cereal is not hearty, nutritious brain food. My wife and I are the nursery leaders at our church every week. I can tell you exactly which of these toddlers have been fed sugar cereal before church based on their poor behavior. (I will now get off my soapbox. Maybe.) I believe in celebrating with food—cookies to celebrate the first snowfall of the year and being taken out to dinner to celebrate the debut of a new book (ahem, darling!)

All that aside, I eat out of the garden because I love it. There is nothing like the flavor, the sense of accomplishment, the joy that comes of growing a garden and then actually eating what you grow. And nothing like seeing the kids and the grandkids garden and eat fresh too—there is a real sense of peace that comes from knowing that the next generations know how to take care of themselves. How do they learn this lost art?

From us. How do they learn that self-reliance is not buying thousands of dollars worth of powdered, dehydrated food that must cause massive depression if you eat if for very long? We have to show them not only how to garden, but how to bring the garden to the table in a way that won't make anyone say "Yuck! I hate vegetables!"

I don't blame anyone who hates vegetables. I agree with them. Those gross, old, pale, disgusting things that have been sitting in metal cans in the grocery store for months are not vegetables. (Not to mention the metal cans lined with estrogen-mimicking plastic, according to recent news reports . . .) Not the ones I grew up with, anyway. Who wants to eat that? if they are from a can, they taste like a can. I've given white sugar beets and golden turnips and rutabaga tastings to hundreds of people,and the people who say "I hate beets" are always surprised to find out that they they there are beets out there in the world that taste great!

I raised turkeys as a youth. When my father and I took the turkeys to the turkey processing plant for, well, processing, I was given a tour. I didn't eat turkey for a decade afterward (no joke). We do kill and eat some of our own chickens, so why I still to this day can't do our own turkey is clearly psychological. But I can't do it. At this writing, we just had one of our backyard cows butchered, and we hired professionals to come and do it (it's a big project, not like doing a little chicken) and I watched. The meat will be ready to pick up in a few days, and I cannot lie, that first delicious meal might not be easy for me. Everyone else in the family is not as tender-hearted as I am. They are all sharpening their proverbial forks and knives. So no, we don't raise turkeys, just because I know I couldn't butcher one and then eat it. I love turkey on Thanksgiving. If we grow our own, I would be the only one at the table who wouldn't be able to eat it. And I'd be the one that did all the work, including the butchering. Not fair! So we buy frozen turkeys, just like everyone else.

We have some special holiday traditions. It might be a bit "Little House on the Prairie" but I think special occasion meals should have at least some totally homemade elements. For example, in recent years we've been having Thorrablot Mash for Thanksgiving and Christmas when we are at home (and not at relatives' homes). You will find that recipe in this book. I was especially proud the year we had fresh Brussels sprouts from the garden for Thanksgiving. I don't think anyone noticed that it took me 45 minutes to peel them all. I try to always make pumpkin pie for both Thanksgiving and Christmas with our own home-grown pumpkins. The secret to this, I have found, is to do a batch of four pies at once, a week or two before Thanksgiving, and then freeze the unbaked pies with uncooked filling inside them. The night before both holidays, I pop the frozen pies into the oven. I try to make my own crusts, but if life is out of control, I buy them pre-made. I like to have glazed carrots from the garden for special meals. I try to freeze some green beans (I've never canned them–takes too long) for special meals.

Q: Do you ever go out to eat?

A: Yes! After all, what's the point of being self-sufficient except saving up enough money to go on vacations and to eat out sometimes? I love a good restaurant. I have a favorite sandwich at the local bakery-cafe. There is a French bakery about 45 minutes from my house, owned by a genuine, French-speaking patisserie chef and his mother, and I am a regular customer, especially for croque monsieur. Occasionally, we go to a fast food restaurant. We are partial to In-N-Out Burger. We order in pizza occasionally, but not nearly as much as I make homemade pizza from scratch with natural yeast dough and sauce from my own tomatoes. I have a weakness for a certain milkshake at a locally owned burger joint. I like food, what can I say? I should add that my wife frowns on all of this. To her, eating out is a massive waste—we could be home having hard-boiled eggs. (She really feels that way. I'm not being facetious.) So going out to eat is almost always my idea.

Q: Do we really eat self-sufficiently?

A: I continue to be asked this question: Do you really eat self-sufficiently? So I wrote a blog post about it at CalebWarnock.blogspot.com. Here it is:

It's a fair question. After all, I wrote the book on it. *The Forgotten Skills of Self-Sufficiency Used by the Mormon Pioneers* is not a research-based book. This is how we live. We eat off our acre and

a half every day of the year, no matter the season. It's not hard, it's not time consuming, and it certainly saves us huge amounts of money. Tastes great!

Someone asked me to tour their garden recently and give them some advice. While they were showing me their spread, this person said to me "It must be nice to stay home all day gardening and researching for your next book."

Um, so wrong.

I have a full-time job (journalist) and several part-time jobs (teaching writing both in person and online classes, book writing, directing conferences, selling pure, non-hybrid seed at SeedRenaissance.com, teaching gardening and homemade yeast and forgotten classes). I'm one of the few lucky people who not only gets to do exactly what I love every day (garden, write, teach) but I am also over-employed in an under-employed economy. (Don't mistake that for well-paid. If you knew what writers get paid, you'd weep. There is a reason we are self-sufficient.)

So no, I don't have luxuriant free time to lounge around gardening and cooking and researching books. This is just our life. I was paid one of the highest compliments of my life this week when a friend looked at me and said "You are the epitome of 'If you need something done, ask a busy person.'" Made my day.

I say all of this because everyone can do something to feed themselves, no matter your

schedule or where you live–a huge farm, a couple of acres, a condo, or a rented apartment. I have lived in all of these, and I have grown my own food on all of these properties to some degree. If you want to do it, you can.

Here is some of what we ate this week:

Pasta sauce

In this dish, I used the following from our garden: onion, carrot, beet, tomatoes, basil, Japanese purple mustard, Swiss chard. I diced the onions, removed the stems from the mustards and chard, grated the carrot and beet and put the tomatoes whole, with all the rest, into the blender with salt for a few minutes and then put the purée on the stove on the lowest possible heat for about an hour and half. We are actually eating this tomorrow, for Sunday dinner over whole wheat pasta, so the sauce is in the fridge as we "speak."

Pizza

In this dish, I used dough made from homemade, natural yeast, sauce made from our tomatoes and basil (puréed and simmered for an hour with salt; I should have put in one of our onions, but I forgot). Also worth mentioning–artisan cheese made locally at Heber Valley Artisan Cheese, which I love!

Cream Stew

In this stew , I used the following from our garden: purple podded pole beans (dried, grown from our own seed), contender beans (dried), white, yellow, orange and red carrots, turnip, and corn.

Garden Salad

In this salad, these vegetables came from our garden: a gourmet lettuce blend of Rouge Grenbloise (a red lettuce), Green Jewel Romaine (grown from our own seed), Oak Leaf (light green and frilly), Merveille de Quatre Saison (bronze and green lettuce); also, orange and yellow carrots.

Toast & Eggs

This dish comprised fresh eggs and toast from homemade bread made with homemade natural yeast. (Raw honey from my parents' farm deserves a mention.)

Garden Soup

In this soup, the following came from our garden: potatoes (grown from our own seed potatoes), rutabaga, swiss chard, onion, basil, carrots, tomatoes (puréed fresh). Also in this soup: lentils, chickpeas, brown rice, hamburger. No recipe. All garden soups are the same: fill the pot about ⅔ with water, bring to boil, put in veggies, cook, and then season to taste. I added the chard at the last minute.

Toast (several times this week–it's been toast weather)

Using homemade bread baked with homemade, natural yeast, spread with an assortment of our homemade jams and jellies.

Sandwiches

I used homemade bread baked with homemade, natural yeast, and lettuces from the garden.

Omelets

The kids have been demanding these, especially Xander. Made with our fresh, free-range eggs, of course.

Apples

We have apples coming out our ears. I've given dozens away this week. The kids gobble them up off the trees, and Charmayne makes wonderful apple crisp. Tomorrow for a treat we are having gjetost cheese over apple slices broiled for 2 minutes–a new favorite treat that a friend introduced me to. The broiled cheese tastes exactly like caramel on the apples. So good!

Cooking Measurement Equivalents

Cups	Tablespoons	Fluid Ounces
⅛ cup	2 Tbsp.	1 fl. oz.
¼ cup	4 Tbsp.	2 fl. oz.
⅓ cup	5 Tbsp. + 1 tsp.	
½ cup	8 Tbsp.	4 fl. oz.
⅔ cup	10 Tbsp. + 2 tsp.	
¾ cup	12 Tbsp.	6 fl. oz.
1 cup	16 Tbsp.	8 fl. oz.

Cups	Fluid Ounces	Pints/Quarts/Gallons
1 cup	8 fl. oz.	½ pint
2 cups	16 fl. oz.	1 pint = ½ quart
3 cups	24 fl. oz.	1½ pints
4 cups	32 fl. oz.	2 pints = 1 quart
8 cups	64 fl. oz.	2 quarts = ½ gallon
16 cups	128 fl. oz.	4 quarts = 1 gallon

Other Helpful Equivalents

1 Tbsp.	3 tsp.
8 oz.	½ lb.
16 oz.	1 lb.

Metric Measurement Equivalents

Approximate Weight Equivalents

Ounces	Pounds	Grams
4 oz.	¼ lb.	113 g
5 oz.		142 g
6 oz.		170 g
8 oz.	½ lb.	227 g
9 oz.		255 g
12 oz.	¾ lb.	340 g
16 oz.	1 lb.	454 g

Approximate Volume Equivalents

Cups	US Fluid Ounces	Milliliters
⅛ cup	1 fl. oz.	30 ml
¼ cup	2 fl. oz.	59 ml
½ cup	4 fl. oz.	118 ml
¾ cup	6 fl. oz.	177 ml
1 cup	8 fl. oz.	237 ml

Other Helpful Equivalents

½ tsp.	2½ ml
1 tsp.	5 ml
1 Tbsp.	15 ml

MORE FORGOTTEN SKILLS of SELF-SUFFICIENCY

Your ancestors knew how to live self-sufficiently—now you can follow in their footsteps!

Bestselling author Caleb Warnock is back with a new collection of money-saving and healthy-living skills to help your family gain independence and self-reliance. Learn how to

GROW SELF-SEEDING VEGETABLES

BUILD RAISED GARDEN BEDS USING STEP-BY-STEP INSTRUCTIONS

COLLECT WATER FROM RAIN AND SNOW

MAKE YOUR OWN LAUNDRY DETERGENT

FIND WILD VEGETABLES FOR EVERYDAY EATING

Discover these tricks and more from the author of The Forgotten Skills of Self-Sufficiency and Backyard Winter Gardening. You can be a living example of independence for the rising generation, and avoid grocery store prices while you're at it.

Whether you're growing an organic family garden or running a no-nonsense household, More Forgotten Skills of Self-Sufficiency is a must-have guide to becoming truly self-reliant for you and your family.

FORGOTTEN SKILLS

— of BACKYARD —

HERBAL HEALING

and FAMILY HEALTH

KEEP YOUR FAMILY HEALTHY, WITHOUT LEAVING HOME!

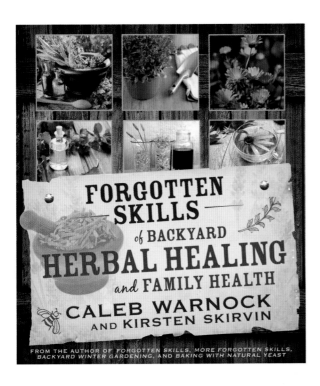

This latest volume in Caleb Warnock's popular Forgotten Skills series teaches you how to grow, harvest, and store your own herbs.

INSIDE YOU'LL FIND

- Tips on how to use specific herbs to treat problems like infections, nausea, acne, and the common cold

- Step-by-step recipes for healing tinctures, medicinal teas, and homemade vinegars

- In-depth guides to common herbs, where to find them, when to pick them, what part of the plant to use, and how to prepare your compounds

- Information about how to avoid common and dangerous mistakes and how to become a responsible herb collector

Let Caleb Warnock and master herbalist Kirsten Skirvin help you take charge of your health care and enjoy the natural benefits of herbal medicine without spending a fortune on artificial pills and supplements. This invaluable book will keep your whole family healthy for years to come!

NOW AVAILABLE AT AMAZON.COM, CEDARFORT.COM, BARNES AND NOBLE, AND OTHER FINE STORES.

TROUBLE'S ON THE MENU

HALLIE DOESN'T BELONG in Tippy Canoe, Montana. She's a California girl used to sunshine and warmth—not cold and snow. But after the unexpected death of her estranged husband, she braves the winter weather to wrap up some of his estate details, only to discover that she doesn't fit in and none of the townspeople like her.

THAT IS, except for the town's handsome mayor, who takes quite an interest in Hallie.

BUT WHEN HIS LIFE starts to spiral out of control, she must decide if he's worth sticking around for in the long term. Join Hallie in this fast-paced, hilarious romance as she learns that sometimes love is the only remedy for a broken heart.

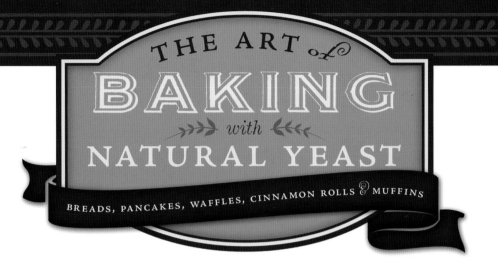

THE ART of BAKING with NATURAL YEAST

BREADS, PANCAKES, WAFFLES, CINNAMON ROLLS & MUFFINS

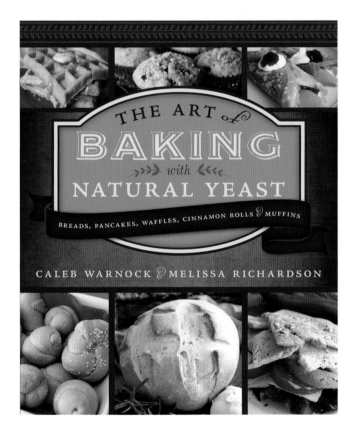

This is the book you've been waiting for! With groundbreaking information about the health benefits of natural yeast, this book will revolutionize the way you bake! Easy to prepare and use, natural yeast breaks down harmful enzymes in grains, makes vitamins and minerals more easily available for digestion, and converts dough into a nutritious food source that won't spike your body's defenses. Improve your digestive health and happiness with these delicious recipes you can't find anywhere else!

BE SURE TO TRY THE:

BLUEBERRY CREAM MUFFINS

QUICK AND EASY CREPES

GARLIC ROSEMARY SOURDOUGH

WHIMSY ROLLS

NO KNEAD BREAD

From quick and easy treats for a busy day to elaborate creations for special events, you'll find something tasty and nutritious to tempt everyone's taste buds!

About the Author

Caleb Warnock is the popular author of eleven nonfiction books and a novel with recipes. He has a master's degree in writing from Utah State University and a bachelor's from Brigham Young University, and he has won more than twenty awards for writing and journalism. Caleb lives with his family on the Wasatch Bench of the Rocky Mountains. He has six stepdaughters and eight grand-children. (There's no "step" between him and his grandchildren.) In his spare time, Caleb relaxes in a hammock strung between an apple tree and a maple tree, overlooking the perennial flowers and vegetable gardens (yes, he has more than one vegetable garden). His blog, Backyard Renaissance, can be found at CalebWarnock.blogspot.com. He sells pure, never-GMO, never-hybrid vegetable seeds (including some of the rarest seeds in the world) at SeedRenaissance.com. You can reach him by email at CalebWarnock@yahoo.com.